Aggie's
family cookbook

Aggie's
family cookbook
Save time, save money

Aggie MacKenzie

PAVILION

To my wonderful sisters – Kerry-Norma, Christine and Karen

First published in the United Kingdom in 2011 by
PAVILION BOOKS
10 Southcombe Street, London W14 0RA
An imprint of Anova Books Company Ltd

Commissioning Editor: Becca Spry
Cover design: Georgina Hewitt
Design: Pene Parker
Photography: Chris Terry
Food Styling: Emma Marsden
Prop Styling: Lisa Harrison
Editor: Susan Fleming
Production: Laura Brodie
Indexer: Hilary Bird

ISBN: 9781862059313

A CIP catalogue record for this book is available from the British Library.

10 9 8 7 6 5 4 3 2 1

Colour reproduction by Mission Productions, Hong Kong
Printed and bound by L.E.G.O. SpA, Italy

www.anovabooks.com

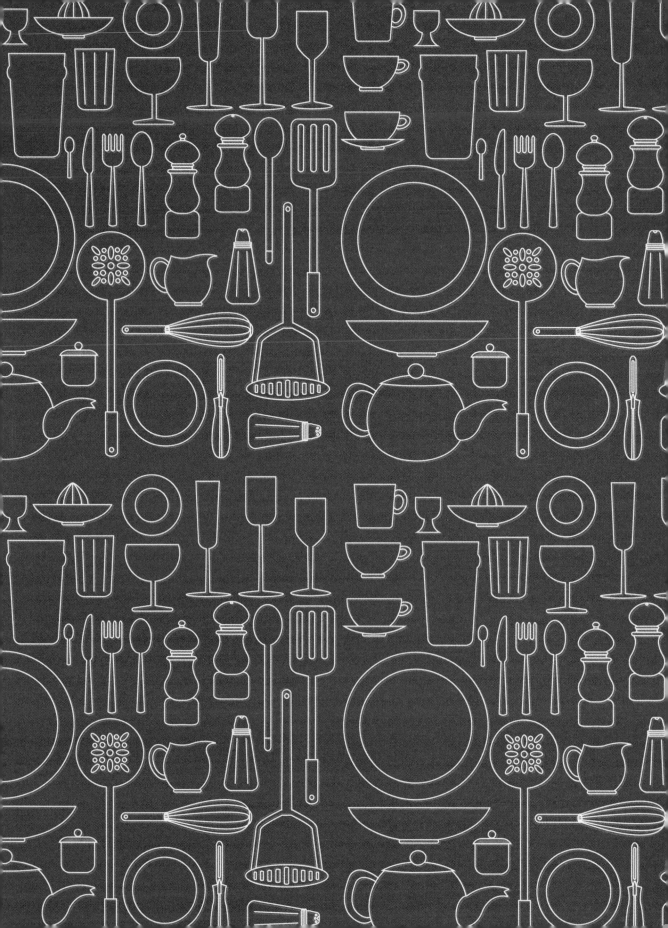

Contents

Introduction

The joy of cooking

There is nothing in this world that makes me happier than cooking for my family – both immediate and extended – and special pals. Eating together and enjoying shared food made with love and good ingredients forms the basis of a life worth living. This collection of favourite recipes I and my family have enjoyed cooking and eating over the past 30-odd years is something I have wanted to put together for a long time.

I came to cooking quite late. Because I passed the 11-plus, I did Latin instead of domestic science at secondary school and so never had the opportunity to learn to cook. Mum ran a tight ship in her very small kitchen, turning out lunches and dinners for six people single-handedly every day. I didn't properly appreciate her broths, stews and scones until I left home. So when I came to work in London in the mid-1970s, aged 20, I realized that if I wanted to enjoy the standard of food I grew up with, and occasionally feed others, I had to cease opening tins of mince and actually learn how to bring ingredients together to form a meal.

I enrolled at a local authority haute cuisine (it was the 1970s, remember!) evening class around the corner from where I lived in south London. The teacher, Mrs K (her husband had a hard-to-pronounce Polish surname), had worked in Claridge's in the war as a pastry chef and her knowledge and

Handy hints for the modern cook
The many years that I've spent working around professional cooks has meant I've picked up masses of useful hints and tips, which I'm shamelessly passing on – for example, how to menu-plan, great ways of stretching a meal to feed extra people, the essential gadgets, and what to have in your storecupboard and fridge (and what not to bother with). When using this book, it's important to use measuring spoons to ensure accuracy.

experience were truly inspiring. That evening class was the highlight of my week; Mrs K became my mentor and I was teacher's pet. She showed us how to make pasta, bone a whole chicken, prepare crab, turn out perfect choux. It was like falling in love. I became completely besotted with everything food-related: cooking, eating, reading, entertaining, the gadgets. When I moved to north London I carried on at Mrs K's evening class for another year, despite the three bus journeys involved in getting home afterwards, with just-cooked chicken chasseur or beef bourguignon in my basket. I used to enjoy surreptitiously lifting the lid off the casserole dish and waiting about 10 seconds until someone further down the bus would turn to their neighbour to say, quizzically: 'Hey, did you get that amazing smell?' That still tickles me now.

There's nothing like a class or course to renew your interest in, and enthusiasm for, cooking. I've attended a fair few over the years and I'd say every time I've felt inspired and invigorated. No matter how experienced a cook you are, there are always new things to learn. The key is to nail your special interest – whether it's pasta- or bread-making or fish cookery – then do a little online research to seek out a specialist course and treat yourself. Lots of cookery schools sell gift vouchers, so make a note to put some on your Christmas list. You will come away with new knowledge and a fresh perspective. For years I was employed producing food-orientated magazines – working with, among others, Nigel Slater, Delia Smith, Anna del Conte, Simon Hopkinson and Ruth Watson – and eventually became head of the Good Housekeeping Institute. Although I wasn't hands-on in the kitchen, I worked

about until mould forms, when they're consigned to the bin. I know, too, how important it is to give accurate recipes – I've bought enough cookbooks over the decades to suss that not all published recipes are properly tested. It's both infuriating and insulting for the buyer and reader.

I've been a working mum for 20 years, so I know all about the importance of getting nutritious, well balanced, exciting and enticing platefuls of food on the table without too much fuss, bother or expense … and without ever having to resort to ready meals.

When my son Ewan was much younger, he said to me, 'Why can't we ever have Domino's; why do we always have to have homemade pizza?' The funny thing is, he wouldn't thank me now for a home-delivery pizza. So something's worked!

I know all about the importance of getting nutritious, well balanced, exciting and enticing platefuls of food on the table without ever having to resort to ready meals.

alongside the cookery team deciding which recipes we would run in the magazine and, trust me, I was always first in line when it was time to taste.

Because I stayed for so long at Good Housekeeping I understand the need for accuracy, how to balance flavours and ensure value for money. It matters, for instance, that recipe ingredient quantities correspond to supermarket pack sizes, so that everything is used and there are no annoying bits and pieces hanging

I hope you enjoy every minute of cooking with this book.

Aggie

What'll we eat this week?

Shopping for good nutrition

Make either carbs or protein the base of each dinner you cook. So if your base is carbs, one night could be rice, another pasta, another potato. Or if your base is protein, one night chicken, another pork, another pulses, and so on. You get the picture.

Once you've decided on the carbs and protein, add in the vegetables. I buy a basic selection every week and always have a bag of frozen peas handy for when the fresh stuff is finished. Sometimes it can be difficult to use up bits and pieces of veg, but the answer is to make what's now become one of my favourite suppers (Baked chicken casserole on page 88).

If you've never written a weekly menu plan before, it could seem a bit daunting. Yet working out what you and your family will eat from week to week – or even month to month – will make life easier and save you time in the long run.

Nor does it mean you have to be a slave to the kitchen. Even though I love to cook, I'm not in there every night turning out restaurant-style meals. Careful planning, making good use of the freezer and stocking the cupboards and fridge so that there's always something to hand is the key. It's that easy.

Here are a few pointers before you put pen to paper.

Decide which day will be the first of your week

What about making Sunday day one? That way, you can cook something substantial for the main meal and, while you're at it, prepare a couple of dishes for the coming week and pop them in the freezer.

Keep the eating plan flexible

There are always going to be nights when you can't predict how many people will be eating – when someone goes out (hold the extra for lunch the following day) or it makes sense for a pal to stay on for supper, for instance. With a cleverly stocked cupboard, you can always

increase the quantity of carbs or add a tin of beans to a stew to get round this. Alternatively, slice meat more thinly.

Stick to your budget

A newspaper feature recently asked whether it is possible to feed a family of four for £50 a week. The general attitude from the food writers responding was that while it is certainly feasible, life wouldn't be a huge bundle of fun, mainly because you would be severely restricted in your choice of ingredients. But while you don't have to be so drastic in your budgeting, it's good to have an element of frugality in your approach.

'Meat-free Monday', an idea that was born out of helping to combat global warming, is a very good starting point to keeping down costs.

Think about the season

You'll probably find that you can stick to the same plan for a couple of weeks, then all of a sudden the weather changes and different ingredients are needed. Summer means lots of fresh salads, thrown together with a quickly griddled chicken breast or halloumi cheese, so there's really no need for the oven. In the winter, the pressure cooker gets pulled out about once a week in my house and I'll make double quantities of stews and freeze half to fill a gap in the following week's plan.

Be prepared for changing plans

There's always going to be the odd day when everyone wants to eat at different times. For emergencies my boys' default option is a bacon sandwich, so that's something I have the ingredients in for at all times. I also like to keep dough in the fridge. It'll be fine for three to four days and it's great just to cut off a piece, roll it out and in a few minutes have a hot flatbread to go with hummus and salad.

Make a basic shopping list

Put all the essentials on your list. I write ingredients under subtitles: fruit and veg, meat, fish, dairy and eggs, storecupboard. Keep this to use every week, then add the extras to it. Write down all your favourite meals to start with and see how they fit together. You'll soon find that you have more than enough to last you a fortnight.

Have a night off once a week

Cook something that can be ready in 15 minutes, such as a frittata, omelette or fresh pesto for pasta (see page 82).

Go veggie one night a week

A stew or a big chunky soup made with lentils or canned beans is much quicker to cook than the meat equivalent – and very healthy too.

Sunday

Sunday-best pork fillet with
special boulangère potatoes
page 155

Monday

Stir-fry with a spicy sauce
(using leftover finely chopped pork
from Sunday instead of prawns)
page 122

Tuesday

Rory's quick steak with watercress
and a hot horseradish dressing
page 128

Wednesday

Kerry's polenta with
mushroom sauce
page 118

Thursday

My Irish stew – in a dash
page 127

Friday

Baked chicken casserole
page 88

Saturday

Matthew's meatballs with
homemade pasta
page 163

Shopping List

Larder

200g/7oz medium egg noodles
200g/7oz/1 cup 1-minute polenta
(cornmeal)
Pearl barley
Matzo meal
Sesame seeds

Fresh

600g/1lb 5oz pork tenderloin
1 bacon rasher (strip)
450g/1 1lb beef mince
2 x 250-300g/9-10½oz rib-eye steaks
2 lamb neck fillets (450g/1lb
total weight)
1 whole small chicken, jointed,
or 8 thighs (skin on)
200g/7oz peeled raw prawns (shrimp)
4 medium eggs
250g pack of butter
100g/3½oz/1¼ cups Parmesan
Crème fraîche
1 lemon, 1 lime
½ aubergine, ½ head of broccoli,
5 carrots, 1 celery stick, ½ fennel
bulb, a handful of green beans,
1 leek, 1 red (bell) pepper, 1 red
chilli pepper, ½ squash, 1 tomato
150g/5½oz watercress
400g/14oz mushrooms
7 onions
2 garlic bulbs
6 potatoes, 2kg/4½lb waxy potatoes,
small bag of new potatoes
Fresh bay, parsley, rosemary, thyme
Fresh root ginger
Crusty bread

Shopping List

Larder

200g/7oz medium egg noodles plus
  2 bundles

400g/14oz dried linguine

400g can chickpeas (garbanzo beans)

Sesame seeds

Fresh

3 slices prosciutto

500g/1lb 2oz beef mince

1.25-1.5kg/2¾lb-3lb 5oz chicken

200g/7oz peeled raw prawns (shrimp)

1 large egg

250g pack of butter

100g/3½oz/1¼ cups Parmesan

Plain yogurt

½ aubergine, 2 beefsteak tomatoes,
  ½ head broccoli, 2 carrots, 1 celery
  stick, 2 handfuls of green beans,
  1 iceberg lettuce, 2 plum tomatoes,
  1 red (bell) pepper, 1 red chilli pepper,
  2 spring onions (scallions), 1 tomato

3 onions

1 red onion

1 garlic bulb

950g/2lb 2oz floury potatoes

Fresh basil, bay, coriander (cilantro),
  parsley, rosemary, sage, thyme

1 lemongrass

Fresh root ginger

1 lime, ½ lemon

4 burger buns

Sunday

Fantastic roast chicken
(save the carcass and leftovers for
Tuesday night)
page 142

Monday

Instant fresh pesto with pasta
page 82

Tuesday

Rory's Asian chicken noodle soup
page 142

Wednesday

Stir-fry prawns with a spicy sauce
page 122

Thursday

The ultimate veggie curry
page 85

Friday

Real burgers
page 72

Saturday

No-hassle gnocchi with sage and butter
page 60

The shopping lists assume you have certain
storecupboard basics. See page 252 for a list of these

Sunday

Make one, freeze one lasagne, with salad (freeze one lasagne for the following week)
page 77

Monday

Ewan's chicken fried rice
page 119

Tuesday

Crowd-pleasing pasta sauce
page 126

Wednesday

Take-anywhere Spanish omelette, with salad
page 175

Thursday

Restaurant-style creamy fish stew
page 120

Friday

Woodfired pizza
page 100

Saturday

Harissa chicken and vegetable tagine
page 148

The shopping lists assume you have certain storecupboard basics. See page 252 for a list of these

Shopping List

Larder

225g/8oz/generous cup long grain rice
20 no-cook lasagne sheets
400g/14oz pasta, such as conchiglie
400g can chickpeas (garbanzo beans)
200ml/7fl oz tomato passata
50g/1¾oz flaked almonds
100g/3½oz dried apricots
50g/1¾oz each of dates and sultanas
1 tbsp harissa paste
3 tbsp oyster sauce

Fresh

6 Italian-flavoured sausages
4 bacon rashers (strips)
Italian pepperoni
700g/1lb 9oz beef mince
1 x 1.5kg/3lb 5oz chicken plus 3 chicken breasts
400g/14oz firm white fish
300g/10½oz salmon
150g/5½oz peeled raw prawns (shrimp)
6 large eggs
1 x 250g pack of butter
250g/9oz mozzarella
125g/4½oz/1½ cups Parmesan
300ml/10fl oz/1½ cups of double (heavy) cream
100ml/3½fl oz/½ cup crème fraîche
1.4ltr/2½pt/6¼ cups milk
½ aubergine, ½ butternut squash, 1 carrot, 1 celery stick, a few chestnut (cremini) mushrooms, 1 courgette, 2 leeks, 1 red (bell) pepper, 1 red chilli pepper, salad leaves, 1 bunch of spring onions
2 shallots, 4 onions, 1 red onion
1 garlic bulb
600g/1lb 5oz potatoes
Fresh basil, bay, coriander (cilantro), flat-leaf parsley, thyme
Fresh root ginger
2 unwaxed lemons, 1 lime

Shopping List

Larder

250g/9oz/1⅓ cups Thai jasmine rice

1 tbsp Thai green curry paste

400ml can coconut milk

2 x 400g cans cannellini or haricot beans

15g/½oz pumpkin seeds

Thai fish sauce

Fresh

900g/2lb pork shoulder, boned

1.2kg/2¾lb gammon joint

4 chicken thighs, skinless and boneless

4 x 150g/5½oz firm white fish fillets,
    such as line-caught cod or pollock

1 medium egg

1 x 250g pack of butter

75g/2¾oz/1 cup Parmesan

150g/5½oz/2 cups cheese such as
    Cheddar, Gruyère or Parmesan

2 tbsp plain yogurt

500-600ml/18-20fl oz/2¼-2½ cups milk

1 small head of broccoli, 1 small head
    of cauliflower, a handful of mangetout
    (snow peas) or sugar-snap peas,
    2 heads pak-choi (bok-choy), ¼ red
    cabbage, 1 red (bell) pepper, ½ red
    chilli pepper, salad leaves, 3 spring
    onions (scallions)

2 onions

1 red onion

1 garlic bulb

1kg/2¼lb sweet potatoes

900g/2lb new potatoes

4 medium potatoes

Fresh flat-leaf parsley, Thai or regular
    basil

1 apple, 2 limes, 2 mangoes

Crusty bread

Sunday

American-style baked ham and beans
(save half the ham for Tuesday night)
page 158

Monday

A great veg dish for leftover cheese
(serve with bread and salad)
page 116

Tuesday

Cold ham with hasselback potatoes
and coleslaw
page 159

Wednesday

Shortcut Thai green chicken curry
page 124

Thursday

Healthy fish and chips (take the
lasagne out of the freezer to thaw)
page 64

Friday

Lasagne (serve with salad)
page 77

Saturday

Diner-style pulled pork with sweet
potato wedges and mango salsa
page 106

Save time, save money at home

Prep ahead to avoid the need for ready meals

Try to prepare one thing on a Sunday that will make your life easier during the week. And if you're chopping an onion, say, do one more at the same time and either freeze it or keep it in the fridge in a sealed container. If you're doing mashed potato, make double and freeze half. Thaw and use as a topping for fish or shepherd's pie. (A woman I used to babysit for in my teens would peel a few days' worth of potatoes in one go, then store them in water in her pantry.)

When I was growing up my mother cooked virtually everything from scratch, and we knew what day of the week it was by what we were eating. The weekly meal plan rarely changed. Sunday was roast beef, and on Monday Mum would make a curry that involved a cooking apple, curry powder and sultanas (golden raisins). She cooked potatoes as well as rice because my dad 'had to have' potatoes every night of the week.

Sunday roast leftovers

* If you have a Sunday roast, you should be able to get two meals out of it. The roast chicken recipe on page 142 shows how to make a yummy soup from the chicken for another night. Otherwise stir the leftover shreds of chicken into a risotto. Here are some more ideas for using up a roast.

* My mum used to make rissoles from cold roast beef, which are delish. She used a mincer, but I just chop the meat very finely and put it in a bowl with a good dollop of mashed potato, a dousing of Worcestershire sauce, freshly chopped parsley and a small finely chopped onion. Add plenty of salt and pepper and mix together well. Shape into patties, then dip in flour, then beaten egg, then breadcrumbs or matzo meal (a great breadcrumb alternative). Heat a little oil and a knob (pat) of butter in a frying pan, and fry on each side until golden.

* Cold roast lamb isn't the most appetizing, but if you fry the slices in a little oil with a few cumin seeds and some sliced red onion, it's a lot more interesting. Serve in pitta with a big salad and a little hummus mixed with Greek yogurt and slices of raw red pepper.

* Slice leftover pork thinly and toss in a stir-fry with carrots, pepper and celery (cut into matchsticks) and a handful of beansprouts. Use the stir-fry dressing from page 122. Serve with rice or noodles and basil leaves, torn and strewn over the top.

Although Mum's regime might sound a little regulated, it was an efficient way of feeding a fairly large family.

Make the most of your freezer

Use your freezer to the max. I put all sorts of bits and pieces in there. Bread, cake, egg whites (for meringues), meat (raw and cooked), soups, sauces and curries all freeze brilliantly.

You really need to label everything (don't trust your memory – I guarantee that you will never remember what is what). Be sure to date the label and then check the drawers from time to time so that you're using food in rotation.

Invest in good-quality sealable containers (I love Lock & Lock) in lots of different sizes so you can chill or freeze anything, from a portion of pesto to a panful of chilli. I wouldn't bother with any very large containers, as they take up a lot of room in the freezer and are difficult to fill up.

How to make the most of your freezer

* When you're making a stew or Bolognese sauce, cook double and freeze half. It won't take much more time, saves energy, and there's an effortless supper the next week. I do this with Pork, chickpea and chorizo stew (see page 104), Minestrone (see page 56) and Rory's spicy chilli (see page 110).

* Use the freezer to store home-baked cakes and biscuits. The brownies on page 206 are ready to eat half an hour after coming out of the freezer and double up as a pudding with sliced fruit and a scoop of ice-cream. Hilary's millionaire's shortbread (see page 238) freezes well, too. Cut it into squares and wrap each in greaseproof (wax) paper so you can take out what you need.

* A crumble mix freezes well and you don't need to thaw it before cooking. Just sprinkle it over the fruit and bake as normal.

* Over-ripe apples and pears can be made into a fruit compote and frozen. Just chop, sprinkle with a little sugar and a splash of orange juice and water and flavour with cinnamon. Cook until soft, then mash briefly. Pack in an airtight container and freeze. To bulk it out, add a couple of spoonfuls of sultanas (golden raisins) or raisins. You'll have an instant base for a crumble or pie or it can be stirred into yogurt or served with a plain cake and ice cream.

* Make double portions of pizza dough (see page 100) and either freeze half or keep in the fridge for instant flatbreads. If freezing, portion up singly, wrapped in clingfilm (plastic wrap), so they'll thaw more quickly.

Make the most of your fridge

Check your fridge is set at 5° – any warmer and food will deteriorate more quickly. Arrange the shelves so you can easily see what's in there. Store fruit and veg in the bottom two drawers. Keep the shelf above those for fresh or frozen meat or fish (wrap it well so nothing can drip on to other ingredients). Use the shelf above that for any ready-prepared foods, such as cheese, butter and cooked meats, and use the top shelf for opened jars.

Make the most of your oven when it's on

Put a tray of roasted vegetables under whatever's in there. In the winter use parsnips, potatoes, squash, celery, onions and carrots. In summer, use aubergines (eggplant), peppers, courgettes (zucchini), tomatoes and red onions. A couple of spoonfuls of these vegetables mixed with canned chickpeas (garbanzo beans) or cannellini beans and tossed with pasta, feta and a glug of oil makes a meal. Or reheat it in a microwave and serve with fried fish. The mixture will last in a sealed container in the fridge for up to five days.

Use a pressure cooker for cheap cuts of meat

A pressure cooker is great in autumn and winter, when you want something warming, as it cuts cooking times by at least half, keeps the food fresh-tasting and uses one pan, so there's less washing-up. Oxtail (see my recipe on page 160), pork and ox cheeks, lamb neck fillet and all those other joints that normally take forever to become meltingly tender work excellently here. You can also use less meat and bulk out with pulses – the result will be much healthier as well as being cheaper. Lentils and yellow split peas don't need pre-soaking, but beans such as haricot, chickpeas (garbanzo beans), cannellini and butterbeans do.

Don't throw away good food

For me, it's plain wrong to chuck out good ingredients – it's like flinging money away – so I make a concerted effort to use up everything. I'm always dismayed at the stats on how much food we as a nation waste. I don't take too much notice of use-by labels. There's a big difference between 'best before' and 'use by'. The latter means that it really should be eaten up before this date and applies to foods such as fresh meat, fish and dairy. 'Best before', however, means it will taste better before the date stated, and this is put on vegetables, fruit and packaged foods. Here's where I'll poke and sniff and taste to check. If bread's gone a bit stale, don't throw it away; blitz in a processor for breadcrumbs, then freeze. You can keep adding to the tub after the first lot's been frozen. Bread that's gone dry can be made into croutons – cut into cubes, put on a baking sheet and drizzle with oil, then bake in a medium oven until golden – or spritzed with water then brought back to life by warming through in the oven. Wrap in foil before putting it in as that helps to create the steam to soften it. A stale French baguette can be made into garlic bread.

Packed lunch ideas

These can be an afterthought, which is a shame for those who eat them. Cooking things at the weekend is cheaper than buying sandwiches and doesn't take very long.

✱ Make a bowl of hummus with canned chickpeas, toasted and ground cumin seeds, olive oil and lemon juice. Stuff this in a pitta with sliced cucumber and a few cherry tomatoes one day, then another day put it with breadsticks, chopped carrot and celery sticks. You can vary this by flavouring the hummus with a chopped marinated pepper.

✱ Boil a couple of eggs at the weekend, then mash with a little olive oil, mayonnaise and some chopped herbs the night before you need to make the sandwich. This is nutritious, takes minutes to prepare, can be stored in the fridge for up to three days and won't go soggy.

✱ Mix together a 400g/14oz can each of kidney beans, borlotti beans and chickpeas in a bowl. Add chopped ham or feta, chopped cherry tomatoes, yellow pepper and celery then toss with olive oil and balsamic vinegar.

Save money at the shops

Plan a month's worth of meals

Work out a matrix of recipes for a month and rotate the weeks (see page 14). It's only right that everyone in the family should have a say in what they eat, so it's worth asking for requests. When I was head of the Good Housekeeping Institute, working alongside the cookery team, these monthly meal plans were some of the most successful features. It was easy to see why. Our readers loved the fact that they had a plan made for them that was simple (and inexpensive) to follow, they didn't have to think about it too much, and their families loved the new recipes as well as twists on old favourites. The meal plan needs to be taped somewhere handy such as the fridge door. (See my meal plans on page 18.)

Before you go shopping

For ease, I write down what I plan to cook during any given week (or even better month – see opposite), then I write a shopping list. This helps me focus my thoughts and take into account who is doing what and whether there are evenings when I need to make adjustments. I recommend you do this. Before you write your list, check the cupboards, fridge and freezer and pull forward the ingredients you're going to use that week. Check the contents of your freezer to see if you can use anything up. (Also make sure everything is well sealed – picking up single peas spilt from a bag is not the best use of your time.)

Buying online and locally

A weekly vegetable box will include a good selection of basics. You can normally request more of your favourites or take away the things you're less keen on. It's also a great way of controlling the quantity you buy.

Order groceries online. I find I'm much more disciplined about what I buy as I don't get distracted from my list.

Buying small quantities works for me, so I get only what we need. I like to support local stores as part of my shopping, and in any case for some things they can work out cheaper than the supermarkets. I live in an area with lots of Turkish shops and will always go to my local for huge bunches of parsley and mint, tomatoes on the vine, pomegranates and tubs of creamy yogurt.

Farm shops and independent ethnic supermarkets can be an Aladdin's cave for bargains. I sometimes buy a big net of about 30 onions from my local shop for £1.50, which lasts for ages. Okay, by the time I get through it the last couple are past it, but I think that's allowed…

Plan to eat less meat

Meat or fish doesn't have to be the centrepiece of a meal. There's conclusive evidence linking red meat with bowel cancer, so we should all take the warning and cut down.

It's much healthier – and cheaper – to make more of grains and vegetables and less meat. Besides, I know I'm not alone when I look at a menu and am much more excited by the ingredients of the (often vegetarian) starters than the mains.

Plan to eat soups

Soups made from vegetables in season are amazingly cheap to turn out, especially if you buy mis-shapes or the basics range. Check out your herb and spice collection to deepen the flavour.

Sweet potatoes cook very quickly and most kids I know love them. Just sweat an onion in butter or oil until soft, add the sweet potato chunks and some stock with a pinch of chilli flakes and some cumin seeds, then simmer for around 15 minutes before subjecting to the stick blender treatment. Onion, potato and spinach make a good soup. Use chicken stock for extra flavour. One all-time favourite soup of mine is the Italian

classic Pasta e ceci. It's basically onion, celery, carrot and garlic softened in oil, then cooked with stock, a can of chickpeas (garbanzo beans) and some tiny soup pasta. The added flavour comes in the form of dried chilli flakes, bay leaves and a sprig of rosemary, all topped with extra-virgin olive oil and some grated Parmesan. It's totally delicious and filling and costs next to nothing.

At the supermarket

When you go shopping, buy an extra carton of milk (not whole milk, though, as it doesn't freeze well) and put it in the freezer so you never run out.

It's easy to get drawn in by special offers, but try not to buy 'just in case'. Take a list with you and aim to keep to it. Decide how much you're going to spend on your supermarket trip and stick to that amount. Easier said than done, but have a go and see how it feels.

Steer clear of BOGOFs unless you know you really will use them. The exception I make is for household products such as loo rolls, washing powder and the like.

Cut out salad bags if you're feeding a family. Compared with the price of a head of lettuce, they cost about five times more. And an iceberg, Little Gem (Boston), romaine or cos will last twice as long in the fridge as an opened bag of soft leaves.

It's worth having a good browse in the frozen section of the supermarket. This area often gets overlooked and it's a shame as it has so much more to offer than ice cream, frozen peas and Yorkshire puddings (oh – the extravagance!). Fish is fantastic – particularly prawns (shrimp) – cheaper than fresh, and you can be pretty sure it'll be in the best condition. I also love to store bags of frozen raspberries or blackberries for an instant pud. They're superb value and dead useful for compote, trifle or ice cream.

Grow your own

Check out your local garden centre for unusual seeds. A packet costs less than a couple of pounds, yet for that you can grow enough cut-and-come-again salad to keep you going from late spring to early autumn. If you buy American land cress, it seems to go on for ever! No outside space? Then plant something in a window box.

Cut herbs cost a fortune. For the same price as a pillow of parsley, you can buy a plant that will last you a season. Hardy types such as bay, thyme or rosemary will grow in the ground and keep going year after year. Soft herbs (eg parsley, basil and coriander/cilantro) need to be planted annually.

Joint a chicken

There's a huge mark-up on chicken pieces. Instead, try buying a whole bird, then joint it. Here's how: arm yourself with a pair of sharp kitchen scissors and a knife. Put the chicken on a board and snip off any elasticated string holding it together. Pull one leg away from the chicken and cut down through the skin until you reach the flesh. Cut between the breast and the leg to remove the leg completely. This is made up of the drumstick and the thigh. As you hold it in your hands you can naturally feel a ball-and-socket joint in the middle – cut through the middle of this to separate the two parts. Do the same on the other side to make two drumsticks and two thighs.

Next remove the wishbone – this is at the opposite end of the cavity. You can feel it underneath the fleshy part of the breast meat and you'll just need a small knife to scrape the flesh away to release it. Once that's done, cut the breast away from the carcass. Take the large knife and cut down one side of the breast bone until it reaches the rib cage, then guide the knife slowly between the flesh and the carcass to release the flesh. At the bottom, cut through the ball-and-socket joint of the wing point attached to the carcass. Repeat on the other side.

Make chicken stock

Use the jointed pieces as you like, and then make stock from the carcass. Put it in a pan, cover with about 1.5 litres/2¾pt/ 6½ cups cold water and throw in a quarter of an onion, 1 roughly chopped celery stick, a carrot, a bay leaf and a few peppercorns. Cover, slowly bring to the boil, simmer for about 30 minutes. Strain. For a reduced, richer-flavoured stock, pour it back into the pan and simmer for another 15 minutes or so, uncovered.

The family larder

If you're not careful, kitchen cupboards and the fridge can get overstuffed with all sorts of packs, jars and sorry-looking bits and bobs. With a little organization and self-discipline, you can have a good base for some great meals, which will save you time and money.

Pasta, rice, noodles and grains last for yonks if they're well wrapped and stored in a cool, dry place. It's easy to get carried away and overbuy when there's an offer at the supermarket, but I store just spaghetti and penne, one pack of each, so precious space isn't taken up by lots of half-opened packs. The same applies to rice – basmati, Thai fragrant and risotto are enough. Cracked wheat or couscous mixed with chopped tomatoes and spring onions will lift a simple summer dish of grilled chicken and take minutes to put together. Dried mushrooms will give depth to an ordinary beef stew. Canned pulses are cheap, filling and handy in stews, salads and soups. Cannellini, chickpeas (garbanzo beans) or butterbeans cooked with olive oil, stock and a pinch of dried chilli flakes, then puréed, make a tasty swap for mash. Reach for noodles the night after a roast: stir-fry a handful of chopped veg and toss with noodles and shredded cold meat, then finish with a splash of soy sauce.

Spices stored for months on end go musty and stale. Keep in a cool, dry place and check use-by dates from time to time. Cinnamon, nutmeg (whole – it tastes best freshly grated) and ginger will double up in curries and rich fruit cakes and biscuits. Cardamom pods, chilli flakes, cumin, coriander and turmeric are the main spices in Moroccan and Indian recipes. Buy whole spices where possible and grind in a pestle and mortar for the best flavour. I keep my spices in a drawer with the names written on the jar tops so I can easily find what I'm looking for.

Store **baking ingredients** in large containers. I keep flour (plain or all-purpose, self-raising and granary) in old-fashioned sweetie jars to reduce the risk of weevils penetrating bags. I store my sugars – caster (superfine), soft light brown, demerara and icing (confectioners') – in secure plastic containers. If you have limited space, buy plain (all-purpose) flour only and convert it to self-raising with baking powder: 1 tsp to every 125g/4½oz/scant cup plain (all-purpose) flour to make 125g self-raising. Other basics are raisins, golden syrup (light corn syrup), cream of tartar, baking powder, bicarbonate of soda and vanilla extract. A bar of dark chocolate – anything over 50 per cent – and cocoa powder are useful, too, for brownies and chocolate sauce.

Olive oil is a culinary all-rounder. It's great for frying or making mayonnaise (use half vegetable oil, half olive if you prefer a milder flavour). Vegetable oil such as sunflower or rapeseed is best for deep-frying as it has a higher smoking point so can be heated for longer without burning. Extra virgin olive oil gives great body to dressings but don't waste it on cooking. Sesame oil in salads and stir-fries gives a unique nutty aroma and flavour.

Plain vinegars such as white wine, red wine and cider keep well. Steer clear of those with added herbs – they're gimmicky and can taste stale.

Canned tomatoes, jars of olives, capers, gherkins, marinated peppers and anchovies are storecupboard stalwarts. After opening, transfer tomatoes and anchovies to airtight containers, keep in the fridge and eat within a few days. Use up marinated peppers within two weeks. Olives, capers and gherkins will keep for much longer chilled.

A note about nuts: because they're high in fat, they go rancid quickly, so always keep them in the freezer (you can use them straight from here).

What I always have in the fridge

The essentials for me are milk, butter, cheese (Cheddar and Parmesan), eggs, plain yogurt, goose fat (for those roasties), lemons, parsley, garlic, potatoes, carrots, onions (red and yellow), shallots, celery, tomatoes, a leek and mushrooms. Bacon, chorizo and those rolls of salami that need

slicing and keep forever sit on another shelf. A bottle of maple syrup and tube of tomato purée (paste) are constants (an opened jar seems to fur up quickly). Vac-packed beetroot and halloumi both have very long shelf lives, and although I might not use them very often, it's a comfort to me to know they are there. Halloumi is great sliced thinly, patted in flour and fried in olive oil until golden to go alongside roasted veg.

A few bottles – Worcestershire sauce, Dijon mustard, ketchup, creamed horseradish and chutneys – sit in the door.

Homemade preserves

I can't go a year without making a couple of batches of preserves. For me, the highlights are January for bitter Sevilles, to make jar upon jar of peel-rich tart marmalade (once you're on a marmalade-making spree, it's difficult to stop). July is special for home-grown raspberries to make my four-minute jam (see page 224). And October finishes the year when British apples and pears are picked from the trees for mellow fruity chutney.

Quick larder suppers

Here is a handful of recipes that are easy to make once you have the basics. They're not set in stone – just adapt them to whatever ingredients you have.

* Good-quality tinned tuna, preserved in oil, makes a great base for a quick lunch. Drain, reserving the oil, then put in a large bowl with a can of drained kidney beans, chickpeas (garbanzo beans) or cannellini beans. Add a little finely chopped red onion and some freshly chopped parsley. Whisk together 2 tbsp reserved oil with 1 tbsp white wine vinegar and season. Drizzle over and toss everything together.

* Although a couple of rashers of bacon make a bacon butty for one, the same amount chopped finely will provide a supper for four. Here's how: fry the bits in a little oil with a couple of finely chopped shallots for around 5 minutes, until starting to turn golden. Throw in a crushed garlic clove and cook for 1 minute, then add a pinch of dried chilli flakes and a can of chopped tomatoes. Season then simmer for around 15 minutes until thickened. Serve with some pasta.

* My recipe for Savoury rice (see page 236) can be turned into a main event with a few extra bits. While it's cooking, fry some finely chopped chorizo and a handful of sliced mushrooms in a drizzle of oil. Once everything in the pan is golden, add a splash of wine or sherry and allow to bubble up, then stir through the rice and serve with a little chopped parsley if you have it. For veggies, make an omelette with two eggs and season well. Throw over a few chilli flakes if you fancy it hot and any chopped fresh herbs you have to hand – coriander (cilantro), basil or parsley are perfect. Slide the omelette on to a board, roll up and slice thinly, then serve with the rice.

* Italian classic Pasta puttanesca is built on preserved goodies. Tip a can of chopped tomatoes into a pan with a little chilli (dried flakes will do if you don't have fresh), a handful of pitted, chopped black olives and four chopped anchovies. Add a pinch of sugar (it stops the tomatoes tasting 'tinny'), then simmer for 15 minutes. Add a tablespoon of capers and freshly chopped parsley right at the end and serve with pasta.

Essential gadgets

The term 'kitchen gadget' makes my heart sing. I love to make bread dough in my stylish, cream-coloured KitchenAid mixer or squeeze oranges in my cheap little juicer on a Sunday morning. That said, every gadget has to earn its place and space in the kitchen.

✱ KitchenAid mixer (or the redoubtable Kenwood Chef – there's one at every car-boot sale and they last for ever). Just the biz for cake mixture and bread dough – indeed all things farinaceous – and perfect for meringues.

✱ Food processor Makes pastry in seconds. I would not contemplate mixing pastry by hand. Ever.

✱ Stick blender Fantastic for puréeing soups, mixing batter or rescuing a sauce that's turned lumpy. Some come in a set with a mini-blender – well worth getting for chopping nuts or grinding spices.

✱ Citrus press Nothing beats freshly squeezed orange juice. (Apart from maybe adding the juice of a grapefruit.) And if you keep your oranges in the fridge, it tastes even better.

✱ Microwave I don't use it for cooking as such, but it's brilliant for reheating and defrosting quickly. And I have proper custard down to a fine art in the micro – five minutes and no splitting!

✱ Microplane grater One Christmas I included one of these in all my sisters' presents. They're so sharp and effective you have to be careful not to incorporate any of your own flesh in the food.

✱ Pressure cooker I bought my now-tatty but beloved Prestige job from a charity shop about 25 years ago, and it's still going strong. It saves on both fuel and time, and as long as you stick to a few simple rules there's nothing to fear and everything to gain. Particularly suited to cheap cuts of meat and pulses.

✱ Wok Apart from its obvious use, it doubles up brilliantly as a deep-fat fryer: good depth with extensive surface area.

✱ Good knives and sharpener Whenever I've asked a chef what his favourite make is, the answer's always different. What they all say, however, is that the knife needs to 'fit' your hand, feel comfortable and have the right weight and balance for you. And the sharper the knife is, the safer it will be, as you'll have less of a struggle to cut. Knives should be sharpened every couple of uses.

✱ Deep freeze Use it efficiently. Label and date everything.

Your capsule kitchen at a glance

Aside from the 'essentials' list, these are what you need to set up a basic kitchen.

Kettle

Toaster

Non-stick frying pan

Ovenproof casserole dish

Baking dish

Roasting tin

Three knives: for chopping, paring and cutting bread

Knife sharpener

Chopping board

Bread bin

Three sturdy saucepans

Three bowls and a silicone scraper

Sieve

Wooden spoons

Colander

Weighing scales

Measuring jug

Peeler

Masher

Rolling pin

Tongs

Tin opener

Corkscrew

Balloon whisk

Lemon squeezer

Ladle

Serving spoons

Pastry brush

Measuring spoons and cups

Cooling rack

Timer

Scissors

Pestle and mortar

Silicone sheet

Not worth the space

* **Breadmaker** I know loads of people who have one and love it, but I feel it removes you so much from the process that it's almost akin to buying a fresh loaf (albeit you don't have to leave the house). I think breadmakers are for people who are afraid of breadmaking. The loaves are air-filled and not particularly authentic, plus the machine uses up so much space.

* **Deep-fat fryer** See Wok.

* **Smoothie-maker** What's wrong with a blender?

* **Cupcake-maker** Call me a grump, but I've never understood the appeal of cupcakes. Sponge, fine, but all that gaggy, gloopy combo of fat and sugar piled on top? They're not long for this world, I'm sure.

* **Any other gimmicky products.** For example, a crêpe-maker, waffle iron, chocolate fountain, electric knives and 'health' grill. I wouldn't give house room to a toasted sandwich maker, but my boys are partial to them.

How to clean your kitchen

The kitchen is certainly the heart of my home – I rarely make it to the living room. Because it's my favourite place in the world and I spend so much time there, I look after it and like to keep it clean (and what would visitors say if I didn't?!).

Cleaning products

You don't need many kitchen-cleaning products. In fact if you're the sort of person who clears up as you go along, you could pretty much get away with washing-up liquid and a cream cleaner for most things. Your mother probably told you this, but it's true: if you wipe up spills immediately, they're much easier to clean. I don't go in at all for antibacterial cleaners. Most bacteria are harmless and necessary for our good health so why would we want to kill them? Overuse of antibiotics in hospitals led to MRSA and we're in danger of going down the same route with antibacterials.

Cleaning schedule

It's a good idea to create a long-term cleaning schedule that lists jobs left out of everyday chores – eg oven, high shelves, insides of cupboards, crumbs in toaster and the like. Do one of these every few weeks and you'll feel very smug.

For a quick once-over, fill the sink with hot soapy water. Using a perfectly clean cloth, wipe down all surfaces, top to bottom, left to right. This includes worktops, cooker hood, fronts of cabinets,

drawers and appliances. Don't forget the handles! Check contents of the fridge, throw out past-it food and wash any drawers or shelves that need it. Clean the sink and taps (faucets), sweep and mop the floor (start in the furthest corner of the room and then work your way towards the door).

Kitchen floor mops can be a bit of a dirty secret...brought out to 'clean' the mucky floor then hidden away again in a dark corner with all the smelly grime clinging to them. I've seen a few specimens in my time. And don't get me started on string mops – putting one of those away clean is a lot more work than doing the floor itself.

A few years ago I was converted to a microfibre mop: you dampen the pad, kept in place with Velcro, which scrubs without any effort, and only water required (so no rinsing). And the best bit is you strip off the pad after use and stick in the washing machine, time and time again, so you'll always have a clean mop to do the cleaning.

If your kids' trainers leave hard-to-shift scuff marks on the vinyl flooring in the kitchen, take a pencil eraser to them (or, better still, get the kids to do it).

Fridge

We're all supposed to pull out the fridge regularly to clean behind, but how many of us do? A good halfway house is to cover a broom handle with a damp cloth, secure with a rubber band and have a good old delve – you might be amazed at what you unearth! If you do decide to go the whole hog, vacuum the cooling elements at the back with the upholstery attachment, then wipe with a soft cloth wrung out in warm soapy water. This will help it to run more efficiently and economically.

If you've cleaned out your fridge and it still has a funny smell (say you've had some prawns in there too long), place a small dish of coffee granules at the back of one of the shelves – they will neutralize any lingering odours. Refresh after a few weeks if you need to.

Dishwasher

The funny thing about dishwashers is that while they may look clean, plenty of gunk can lurk in corners. And the filter! Remove it every week and give it a good wash with a nylon brush in a sink of hot soapy water. Now take a wodge of kitchen paper along the gap where the bottom of the door meets the base of the machine – you could get a nasty shock at the amount of rotting dreck there. Once you've done those bits, throw a cup of vinegar in the machine and run an empty cycle – great for keeping the pipes clear of limescale, too. There's a lot of confusion about those 3-in-1 dishwasher detergents and whether they do away with the need for

salt and rinse aid. Just to be on the safe side, you should always keep those compartments topped up, particularly if you're in the habit of running lower-temperature washes.

Washing machine

Every week I get asked, 'Why does my washing machine smell, even though I leave the door open?' The reason is because we're all washing too often at low temperatures or always using the quick cycle. Bacteria, which produce gases that give off a bad smell, will survive a 30 degree wash, so when the water drains away, the bacteria are left behind to build up and grow in number in the humidity of the machine, hence the nasty niffs (and eventually black mould on the seal). The answer? Do a 'maintenance wash': throw a cup of clear vinegar into the empty drum and run the machine on the hottest wash. Thereafter, make sure you do a 60 degree wash once a week, particularly for towels and cotton sheets. Sweet smells guaranteed from now on.

Thank God for dirty dishes,
They have a tale to tell;
While others may go hungry,
We're eating very well.   (Anon)

Oven

Now the oven … the reason it's minging is because you don't clean it each time you do a roast dinner. If you've left it a while, place an ovenproof bowl of water inside at a high temperature for 30 minutes (the steam will soften the dirt, making it easier to shift). Then get to work with your preferred oven-cleaning product, avoiding contact with any self-clean linings (which are rough to the touch). Wear rubber gloves, ventilate the room well and cover the floor with newspaper for protection. You have to be in the mood for this job and if you think you never will be, get it cleaned professionally and resolve to change your ways radically thereafter. For stubborn bits on oven shelves, rub a piece of fine sandpaper along the lines of chrome then wash with soapy water. After the inside is clean, smear a thin paste of bicarbonate of soda (baking soda) and water on enamel linings (not self-clean), which dries and absorbs grease, making it easier to clean next time. Looks messy but worth it.

And then this happens soon afterwards: you've lovingly made a lasagne or apple crumble and the filling's bubbled over and is a burnt mess stuck to the oven floor. Worry not: all you need to do is sprinkle with dishwasher powder, cover with a couple of sheets of wet kitchen paper, leave a few hours and it'll come off easily with a damp cloth. Don't waste time scrubbing at baked-on grime in a roasting dish. Fill with hot water to cover the stains, add a handful of biological washing powder or a dishwasher tablet, bring to the boil and simmer for about 15 minutes. Leave to soak for a further few hours and then it will come off easily.

The metal grilles in a cooker hood quickly get greasy (and when oily drops start falling on your hob below, you know it's time for action). Most can go in the dishwasher on a hot wash, but if you don't have one give them a good soak overnight in a hot, strong washing soda solution – about a cup of crystals to 600ml/1pt/2½ cups hot water. If they're too big for the sink, stick them in the bath (line with a towel to stop scratches). If they're still a bit greasy renew the solution and get the last of the gunk off with a nylon brush. For burner rings, soak in a sink full of hot, soapy water. This will loosen the dirt and make them easier to clean.

Cupboards

Dust at high levels will be welded on with a layer of grease; the best thing to cut through it easily is a solution of warm water and washing soda – depending on how thick the grease, up to a cup per 500ml/18fl oz/2¼ cups warm water. It's cheap, works like magic and is sold in supermarkets and hardware stores. Afterwards lay a sheet of newspaper on top of high cupboards and replace from time to time (no cleaning required).

Blitz cupboards and throw away any out-of-date flour or nuts (they'll be rancid). Food moths always seem to find their way into old dry ingredients and, once you're infested, it's hard to get rid. Wipe shelves with a clean cloth wrung out in warm soapy water, getting right into the corners, and buff dry. Keep nuts in the freezer and use straight from frozen and buy flour in small quantities.

Taps (faucets)

For limescale on chrome taps (faucets), envelop with vinegary kitchen paper, cover with a plastic bag and secure with a rubber band. Leave overnight and in the morning the scale will flake off. For a furred-up kettle, half-fill with clear vinegar (not malt – it'll go everywhere) and half water. Boil and leave overnight. Repeat if necessary. Rinse and reboil a few times with water before using.

Chopping boards

Wooden versus plastic versus glass chopping board – which is more hygienic? It depends on how well you clean your board. Wood is good as long as it's scrubbed thoroughly after every use with very hot soapy water, then rinsed with hot running water. Never leave it to soak – it'll swell and crack. Dry with paper towels to avoid germs from a used tea-towel. Leave to air, resting on its edge (it can warp if dried flat). To get rid of strong smells, simply squeeze some lemon juice (or sprinkle some mustard powder) on the board and then wipe with a clean damp cloth.

A plastic board can go in the dishwasher, but otherwise treat in exactly the same way. Always use separate boards for raw meat and veg, and replace a cracked or badly scored board, whatever it's made from. Glass is most hygienic as no grooves will form to house food-poisoning bacteria but disastrous for knife blades.

If it's your chosen surface, wipe over with a soapy cloth and dry immediately.

Freezer

Like most women, I'm always in a rush and so when the freezer needs to be defrosted I'm too impatient to wait around for the ice to melt on its own. After I switch off, I unload everything into a binbag then place a large bowl of boiling water inside – the glaciers soon start shifting. If the ice is particularly stubborn, I help it along with a quick burst of the hairdryer – it works wonders! But do make sure the water doesn't drip on to the hairdryer. Once defrosted, the nasty pea-infested water baled out and goodies reinstalled, don't forget to switch back on. After defrosting an upright freezer, wipe down the elements and coat with glycerine – the next defrost will be miles easier.

Microwave

To clean inside a microwave, fill a bowl with water, add a few slices of lemon and run on high for a few minutes. The steam will loosen any baked-on food so you can easily wipe it clean.

Worktops

If the wooden drainer around your kitchen sink has black mould in the grooves, rub with very fine grade wire wool dipped in white spirit. Dry and coat with a mix of one-third boiled linseed oil (from hardware shops) and two-thirds white spirit, using a soft cloth. Leave overnight then remove excess. Do it twice a year to keep wood looking good.

Are your beech worktops looking a bit worse for wear, with lots of rings left by hot cups and glasses of red wine? Here's what to do. Using a damp green scourer, rub a little neat washing-up liquid into the stains then lightly go over it all with some very fine sandpaper (in the direction of the grain) before applying a thin film of oil. Make up a solution with one part boiled linseed oil mixed with two parts spirit. Best to do this before going to bed so the oil soaks in overnight. Thin film, remember – too little is way better than too much. If there's any still sitting on the surface in the morning, wipe with a dry, lint-free cloth.

A granite worktop looks lovely but sometimes the area around the tap (faucet) and sink take on a 'bloom' from mineral deposits in water – and limescale cleaners can be too harsh on a natural surface. Deal with any persistent marks by simply rubbing with very fine wire wool, dampened.

When I worked on 'How Clean Is Your House?' I became very aware of the dangers of allowing cats on kitchen surfaces. Think about it: Kitty comes from her litter tray (we all know what's in there), hops up on to the surface (pad, pad, pad), then a little later along comes someone to make a sandwich. You get the picture. Discourage this from day one!

Teaching the kids to cook

Get children to respect food

While I and my three sisters were growing up, we weren't really welcome in the kitchen while Mum was preparing meals, except maybe on a Sunday to lend a hand with the trifle (which was an assembly job anyway). She had to produce lunch and dinner every day for six people in a very small space so had to work very quickly and efficiently. Little ones mucking in would not only slow up but also mess up the process. So although none of us sisters growing up had much of a clue about how to get a meal on the table, we all inherited a sound culinary code: if you want your body to work well for you, don't stuff it full of rubbish. Mum made everything from scratch and, even at 90, still does to a great extent.

Having a lifelong love of good food and distaste for ready meals (home delivery curries are the exception), it was obvious that my boys were going to be similarly influenced. Matthew, their dad, also loves good grub and is a fabulous cook.

I remember my son Ewan saying to me years ago, 'Why can't we be like other families and have a takeaway, instead of always having to eat homemade food?' He seemed to feel genuinely deprived.

What struck me then (and it's something I appreciate now) is how children's tastebuds develop and it's only by guiding them in the right direction that they'll build up a good repertoire of flavours, textures and variety. It's a drip-drip effect. If either of my children ever said, 'I don't like that' without even trying it, I always insisted that they give it a go first before they could say they didn't actually like whatever it was. And one of the best parts of being a parent is seeing how, with a little persuasion and particularly if they're really hungry, they'll be more willing to try something new.

What struck me then (and something I appreciate now) is how children's tastebuds develop and it's only by guiding them in the right direction that they'll build up a good repertoire of flavours, textures and variety.

Here are some of the ways in which we best managed to get our boys involved in the kitchen and interested in good food.

Start your children cooking early

Get them involved in all aspects of food: shopping, choosing, peeling, mixing, tasting. I have a lovely memory of Ewan standing on a stool so he could be high enough to stir the scrambled egg he fancied for his breakfast. From about four years old they can help with little tasks such as rolling out pastry, podding peas or peeling veg – and even washing up. I've never met a child who hasn't loved splashing around in warm soapy water (warning: you can go through a lot of washing-up liquid this way).

Stay relaxed about mess

Getting their hands in, touching the ingredients, feeling as if they are creating something exciting and spending time together is worth far more than the few minutes needed to clear up the bits later.

Baking brings instant rewards

It's also deeply enjoyable. It can be something as simple as breaking the eggs or stirring the batter for pancakes and helping to fry them in the pan (see recipe on page 216), shaping rolls or rolling out pizza dough. Cakes and biscuits, of course, are an obvious route, and children can enjoy feeling pride in their work as they share the goodies around.

Expose them to different flavours and textures

We've always tried to expose our boys to as many different flavours, textures and styles of cooking as possible. Nothing should be off-limits. Trying new things doesn't have to mean spending lots of money going to fancy restaurants – it could just be a local place, or a stall on a market, that serves good ethnic food that's a bit different. A cookery class is a great route to new food ideas (for adults as well as children). It can give the child a sense of ownership and a real feeling of pride and achievement.

Change your shopping habits

Visiting a farmers' market is so much fun. It's a great way for children to get to understand where food comes from and how it is produced. Plus there are often lots of stalls giving away tasters. Every Saturday, my local farmers' market in Stoke Newington is held in the primary school playground and it's lovely seeing kids jumping off the climbing frame one minute then tucking into a gorgeous-looking sandwich of hot buttery garlicky mushrooms on sourdough the next.

Turn fast food into healthy grub

For instance, burgers, pizza and chips. Show your children how they can be made at home, putting in the best ingredients to create something that is so much more delicious (and a lot healthier) than ready-made versions.

Involve the children in deciding what you're going to eat

But don't, whatever you do, fall into that trap of cooking different things for different people at the same meal. (The words 'rod' and 'back' come to mind.) When Rory and Ewan were younger, we'd always have a chat at the end of every meal about what we wanted to eat the following night. That way, there was always a little bit of excitement already building up for the next supper (not that we were obsessed, of course!).

Prepare meals with the kids

Once a week take some time for one parent and one child to prepare a meal for the rest of the family. There might be a bit of falling out along the way but if you keep it simple and delicious and you're prepared to do all the clearing up if the little one gets bored, it's an easy way of exploring food and making it enjoyable.

Put a foodie spin on parties

For a while pizzas took top billing at kids' birthday parties. All you need to do is knock up a load of dough (see page 100), put the sauce and all the toppings in the middle of the table then let everyone help themselves and build up their own creations. It's great fun, entertaining and there undoubtedly will be a few new interesting food combinations created as well. And less chance of anyone throwing up because they've OD'd on junk.

Grow your own

Grow some sort of edible, herb or salad, in the garden or pot on a window ledge if you don't have space outside. In the summer months, for instance, you can plant rocket (arugula) or lettuce seeds and you'll be harvesting within three or four weeks. I have a patch full of salad every summer. It's great to see one of the boys come into the kitchen for a sandwich then nip out to the garden to snip some stems to tuck into the sandwich. That's my boy.

When they leave home

Rory's at college in Leeds and having to live on a budget. He quickly discovered where the good buys are and how best to use his money. For instance he uses the local market for fruit and veg and scoops up three-for-two meat bargains at the supermarket. He likes nothing better than to organize a big Sunday roast. Everyone contributes towards the cost and he goes off and gets a half-price duck from the supermarket. As I write this Ewan is preparing to start a three-year chef's diploma at Westminster Kingsway College in London.

I do believe it's no small coincidence that they've been brought up in a household that's more than a little preoccupied with food. I'm so looking forward to being cooked for in my dotage.

Recipes

A few favourite classics

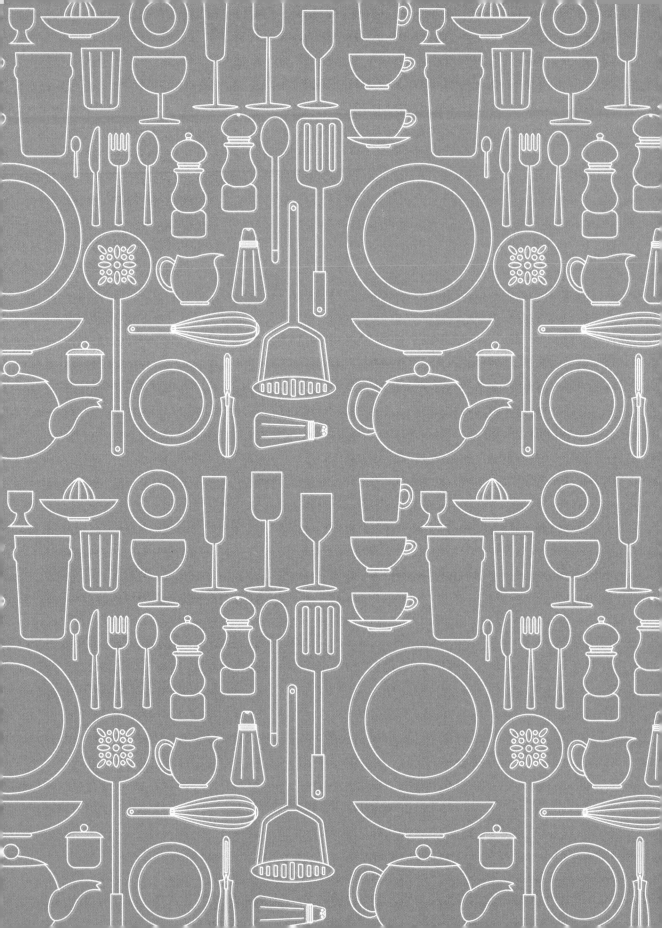

A few favourite classics

Best-ever pumpkin risotto

Years ago I went to a risotto masterclass taught by Valentina Harris at the Italian cookery school, La Cucina Caldesi, in London. She learned from one of the cooks she grew up with in Italy – an old man, I believe, who got her to stand on a stool next to him and watch what he was doing.

Valentina was very precise in her instructions and it's these ones I still follow today. The onion has to be cooked until really soft, then the rice toasted with the softened onions until it lets out a great big sigh, at which point the wine is poured in. Then it's all eyes on the risotto as the stock is added slowly, ladle by ladle, allowing it to be absorbed gradually.

Prep: 15 minutes
Cook: 45 minutes
Serves 4

1 small pumpkin or squash (around 600g/
   1lb 5oz), peeled and chopped into
   bite-size pieces
1 tbsp olive oil
A few sprigs of fresh thyme
4 fat garlic cloves, unpeeled
Salt and freshly ground black pepper
1.2ltr/2pt/5 cups hot vegetable stock
50g/1¾oz/scant ½ stick unsalted butter,
   plus a little extra
1 onion, very finely chopped
350g/12oz/1¾ cups risotto rice
125ml/4fl oz/½ cup dry white wine
Parmesan, to serve

1

1. Preheat the oven to 220°C/200°C fan/425°F/gas mark 7. Put the squash in a large roasting tin and drizzle over the oil. Add the thyme and garlic. Season well. Toss everything together to coat. Roast for 30 minutes, giving the tin a good shake halfway through the cooking time. Next, pour the stock into a pan and heat until it reaches a very gentle simmer.

2. Melt the butter in a large pan. Add the onion and cook it over a lowish heat until soft but not coloured, around 15 minutes. Add the rice.

3. Stir. Cook the rice for up to 8 minutes, ensuring that it is evenly coated with the onion and butter mixture and that it's hot all the way through. You'll begin to hear it squeak and sing. Season well.

4. Pour in the wine – the rice will let out a great big sigh – and stir in. Cook until the wine is all absorbed.

5. Now this is the bit where you need to be at the hob for a while. Start to add the stock, one ladleful at a time, and stir it in. You need to stir the mixture constantly to allow all the grains of rice to cook evenly. Do not add another ladleful until the last one has been absorbed. The further down the stock you go, the longer it will take for the last few ladles to cook in.

6. When the last ladle of stock has almost been absorbed, throw over the remaining knobs of butter, season again and add most of the pumpkin or squash.

7. Stir, then grate over some Parmesan. Leave to sit for a few minutes. Spoon into bowls, add the remaining pumpkin or squash and a garlic clove, and let people help themselves to more Parmesan.

5

6

7

Clever cooking

~ If you have a roasting tin where everything sticks to the bottom, simply line it with baking parchment and the veg will come out easily.

Also try this...

~ This can easily be a storecupboard supper if you don't have any squash. Just throw in a couple of handfuls of frozen peas with the last ladleful of stock instead.

~ For a springtime risotto, stir in four asparagus spears, steamed and chopped, and a handful of cooked fresh peas with a sprig each of fresh mint and basil, chopped.

New Year's Day minestrone

I like to have a gathering at home on New Year's Day (you can take the girl out of Scotland…), and this is fantastic for chasing away a hangover. It's good for vegetarians, but has enough body with the beans for meat-lovers.

Prep: 30 minutes
Cook: around 2 hours
Serves 4 generously

1 tbsp olive oil
1 onion, finely chopped
2 carrots, diced
2 celery sticks, diced
½ fennel bulb, diced
125g/4½oz dried cannellini beans,
  soaked overnight in cold water
400g/14oz canned chopped tomatoes
1 tbsp tomato purée (paste)
1 bay leaf
1 sprig fresh thyme
1 tsp powdered vegetable stock or
  1 vegetable stock cube
¼ savoy cabbage, shredded
A handful of small soup pasta
Parmesan, to serve

Heat the oil in a large saucepan and sauté the onion, carrot, celery and fennel for a good 10-15 minutes until softened and starting to turn golden.

Drain the beans and add to the pan with the tomatoes, tomato purée (paste), bay leaf and thyme, then pour in 1.2ltr/2pt/5 cups boiling water. Give everything a stir, cover and bring to the boil, then reduce the heat to a simmer and cook for 1½ hours, or until the beans have softened.

Stir in the stock, cabbage and soup pasta and then continue to cook for around 10 minutes, or the time stated on the pack of pasta.

Divide among soup bowls and grate over a little Parmesan, offering extra should anyone fancy more.

Also try this...

~ If there are leftovers, chill in an airtight container. As time goes by, it gets thicker but you can easily water it down and it will still taste great.

~ If you're looking for a way to use up the half fennel, turn to page 155 and try my twist on boulangère potatoes with fennel and onion.

Save time

~ Knock an hour off the cooking time by making this in a pressure cooker. After adding the water, cook on low pressure for 30 minutes. Release the pressure and complete recipe.

Ewan's tempura with crispy bits

My son Ewan loves experimenting in the kitchen and the first time he tried this it worked perfectly. It's best to use veg that cooks quickly in the hot oil and that you can eat with a little bit of bite if you happen to undercook it. Here's our favourite combination below.

Prep: 15 minutes
Cook: 15-20 minutes
Serves 4

4 slices aubergine (eggplant), quartered
At least 2ltr/3½pt vegetable oil
2 medium carrots, cut into thin pieces
A handful of green beans
A handful each of cauliflower and broccoli
   florets, halved if large
½ red (bell) pepper, sliced

For the tempura batter
120g/4¼oz/scant cup plain (all-purpose)
   flour
40g/1½oz/¼ cup cornflour (cornstarch)
200ml/7fl oz/scant 1 cup sparkling water
Salt

For the dipping sauce
2 tbsp soy sauce
1 tsp sweet chilli sauce
1 tbsp sesame oil
1 tsp white wine vinegar

Also try this...
~ Feel free to experiment with the veg –
baby corn is good too – but we've found
that spring onions (scallions) go soggy,
and sweet potato takes a long time to
cook unless you chop it into very thin
pieces.

For the batter, sift the flours into a bowl and pour in the sparkling water. Whisk briefly – it doesn't need to be super-smooth. Season with salt and set aside.

Lay the aubergine (eggplant) quarters on a plate and cover with salt. Meanwhile, mix together the dipping sauce ingredients in a small bowl and set aside.

Heat the oil in a large deep pan until hot. It's ready when you throw a crumb of bread into the pan and it sizzles madly. Watch it all the time for safety.

Line a large flat baking sheet with kitchen paper. Arm yourself with two large metal spoons – one to drop the coated veg into the pan and another to scoop it out (a slotted metal spoon is perfect for that bit).

Add a few chopped vegetables (not the aubergines/eggplant) to the batter and toss to coat each piece. Start to spoon the pieces into the oil – you can fry about four at a time. Cook until crisp and just starting to turn golden. Lift out and drain on kitchen paper. Do the same with the rest of the veg, saving the aubergine (eggplant) until last (just brush off the salt before coating in the batter). Keep lifting out and draining the crispy blobs of batter at the edge, too. Spoon it all on a big plate, with any crispy bits, and put the sauce alongside.

No-hassle gnocchi with sage and butter

I love gnocchi. The supermarket stuff is a good storecupboard standby, but this is a lot of fun to make, the ingredients are basics and I always have them in.

Prep: 30 minutes
Cook: 20 minutes
Serves 4

600g/1lb 5oz floury (starchy) potatoes, unpeeled
Salt and freshly ground black pepper
1 large egg, beaten
175g/6oz/1¼ cups plain (all-purpose) flour, sifted

To serve
75g/2¾oz/⅔ stick unsalted butter
About 12 small fresh sage leaves
Parmesan

clever cooking

~ A potato ricer is great for this as it keeps the dough light. If you mash the potato with a masher, it tends to make it gluey and the gnocchi heavy.

Also try this...

~ These gnocchi are delicious tossed through the Easy-peasy tomato sauce on page 237, or the Bolognese on page 75.

1. Prick the potatoes all over and then place in the microwave. Cook on high for around 12 minutes until tender, turning them halfway through. The potatoes will be boiling hot when they come out, so use a clean tea-towel to pick them up and protect your hands while you peel away the skin with a sharp knife. Press them through a potato ricer into a bowl.

2. Season with about a teaspoon of salt, and then quickly stir in the egg.

3. Add half the flour and mix again.

4. Tip on to a board with the remaining flour. Quickly knead in as much flour as the dough will take. Keep going until it's firm.

5. Bring a large pan of water to the boil. Add 1 tsp salt. Divide the dough into four pieces. Roll one out to make a thin sausage shape.

6-7. Cut off 2.5cm/1in gnocchi on the diagonal.

8. You can mark the top of each gnocchi with a fork if you like. Do the same with another of the four pieces of dough.

Put all these little uncooked gnocchi on a plate and gently tip them into the pan. They'll drop to the bottom, but after a few minutes they will start to bob to the top. While they're cooking, roll out and cut the other two pieces of dough in the same way.

Lift the gnocchi out of the water with a slotted spoon and put on a plate. Cook the second batch.

While that's cooking, melt the butter in a frying pan (skillet), then add the sage leaves. Cook until the leaves are just crisp.

Divide the gnocchi between four plates, then spoon some of the sage and butter over each. Season and grate the Parmesan over the top.

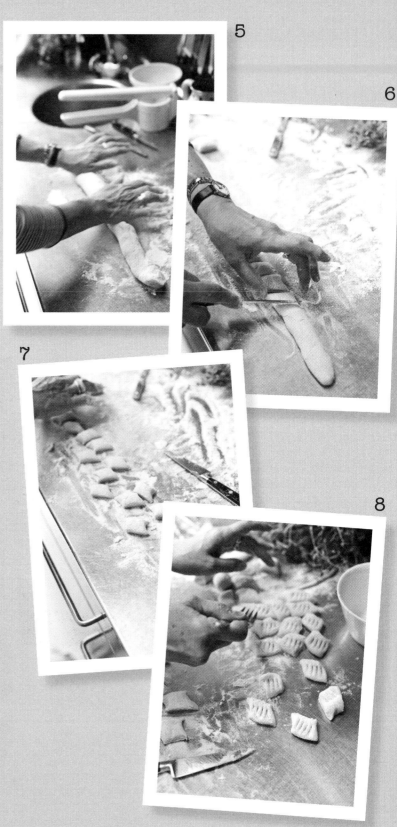

5

6

7

8

Healthy fish and chips

Although there's nothing like fish and chips from a good takeaway, I like to make my own healthier version. I serve it with a generous dollop of piquant tartare sauce on the side.

Prep: 15 minutes
Cook: 40-45 minutes
Serves 4

4 medium potatoes, each cut into 6 wedges
A little olive oil
Salt and freshly ground black pepper
4 x 150g/5½oz firm white fish,
   such as line-caught cod or pollock
250g/9oz frozen peas

For the tartare sauce
1 medium egg yolk
75ml/2½fl oz/a good ⅓ cup each of
   sunflower oil and olive oil
1-2 tsp white wine vinegar
1 spring onion (scallion) or ½ shallot,
   finely chopped
1 tbsp finely chopped fresh parsley
2 cocktail gherkins, chopped
1 tbsp capers

Also try this...

~ To use up the egg white, try Rory's sweet and sour pork recipe on page 70.

Preheat the oven to 220°C/200°C fan/425°F/ gas mark 7.

Put the potatoes into a large roasting tin lined with baking parchment. Drizzle over the oil, then lift each side of the paper up and toss the wedges around to coat in the oil. Spread the wedges out again and season well. Roast for 30 minutes.

Reduce the oven to 200°C/180°C fan/400°F/ gas mark 6. Season the fish, drizzle over a little oil, and put it in a separate shallow ovenproof dish. Cook underneath the potatoes for 10-15 minutes until the fish just flakes when pushed with a knife.

While the fish is cooking, make the tartare sauce. Put the egg yolk in a large bowl and beat well. Start to add the oil, drop by drop, whisking constantly until it's combined with the yolk. It'll start to thicken as you do this. After adding about half the oil, whisk in the vinegar. Continue to add the oil – you can drizzle it in now – still beating well to make sure it's all incorporated.

Stir in the spring onion (scallion) or shallot, parsley, gherkins and capers. Season well.

Cook the peas in a pan of boiling water, following the instructions on the packet. Divide the chips, fish and peas between four plates and then serve with the tartare sauce.

Worth-the-effort Niçoise salad

This speaks of summer to me – my favourite time of year – as it's full of all those Mediterranean flavours that go so well together. It looks really vibrant in the salad bowl and it's healthy, too. It's a bit of a faff to make because you need to cook the potatoes, eggs and tuna separately but the result is so worth it.

Prep: 15-20 minutes
Cook: 15 minutes
Serves 4

For the salad

500g/1lb 2oz new potatoes, halved
A handful of green beans, halved
8 quail's eggs
A little olive oil
Salt and freshly ground black pepper
2 x 150g/5½oz tuna steaks
2 Little Gem (Boston) lettuces
A few caperberries
4 plum tomatoes, quartered
8 canned anchovies, drained of oil
A few sprigs of parsley, finely chopped

For the dressing

1 shallot, finely diced
3-4 tbsp olive oil
1 tbsp white wine vinegar
2 tsp Dijon mustard

Cook the potatoes in a pan of boiling water for 10-12 minutes until just tender. Add the green beans and cook for another 2 minutes until tender. Drain well and cool a little.

Cook the quail's eggs in a pan of boiling water for 2 minutes. Lift out and put in a bowl of cold water. Once cool, carefully peel the eggs.

Drizzle a little oil in a frying pan (skillet), season the tuna, then fry for 2-3 minutes on each side, until still pink in the middle, or done to your liking. Put on a board and slice across the grain into thick fingers.

Layer up the salad ingredients in a large salad bowl. Mix together the dressing ingredients with 1 tsp boiling water – this helps the oil and vinegar combine – and drizzle over the salad. Toss and serve.

Proper Caesar salad

I've called this recipe 'proper' as it's devised from the Caesar salad's true origins. The dressing should be made from a coddled egg and taste creamy with a hint of sharpness from the vinegar and a mellowness from the spike of mustard. Leave the chicken out... it was never meant to be there.

Prep: 15 minutes
Cook: 11 minutes
Serves 4

125g/4½oz day-old bread,
   cut into little squares
2 tbsp olive oil
2 garlic cloves
Salt and freshly ground black pepper
4 Little Gem (Boston) lettuces,
   leaves separated
8 canned anchovies, drained of oil,
   roughly chopped
50-75g/1¾-2¾oz Parmesan, grated

For the dressing
1 large egg
3 tbsp olive oil
2 tsp white wine vinegar
A splash of Worcestershire sauce
A knifepoint of Dijon mustard

Preheat the oven to 200°C/180°C fan/400°F/ gas mark 6.

Make croutons: put the bread in a bowl with the olive oil. Smash the garlic cloves on a board using the flat blade of a heavy knife and add them to the bowl. Season and toss well. Tip into a roasting tin and bake for 10 minutes.

To make the dressing, bring a small pan of water to the boil. Add the egg and cook for 1 minute. Cool under running water, then crack and tip the contents into a bowl, scraping out the just-cooked white from the shell. Add the remaining ingredients for the dressing, then season well and whiz in a blender.

Start to assemble the salad. Put the lettuce leaves in a large bowl and pour over the dressing. Toss well so that all the leaves are coated. Lift up some of the leaves and scatter in the anchovies and some of the croutons, ensuring there's some of each on every layer. Scatter over the Parmesan, toss again, season and serve.

Rory's sweet and sour pork

I came home one day to find my son Rory cooking this, with everything organized and in order on the hob. I was very impressed by the way he was completely in charge of all the ingredients and knew exactly what to cook when. It's absolutely delicious, too!

Prep: 30 minutes
Cook: 30 minutes
Serves 4

225g/8oz/generous 1 cup long-grain rice
Salt and freshly ground black pepper
2 tbsp cornflour (cornstarch)
5 tbsp plain (all-purpose) flour
1 medium egg white
2ltr/3½pt vegetable or sunflower oil
400g/14oz pork tenderloin, cut into
    1cm/½in pieces

For the sauce
1 tbsp groundnut (peanut) oil
1 onion, roughly chopped
½ each of red and green (bell)
    pepper, chopped
1 carrot, sliced
2 tbsp tomato ketchup
3 tbsp white wine vinegar
2 tbsp soy sauce
½ tbsp caster (superfine) sugar
1 tsp cornflour (cornstarch)
227g/8oz canned chopped pineapple in juice

Also try this...

~ To use up the egg yolk, try my recipe on page 64 for Healthy fish and chips.

~ For extra bite, you can add two roughly chopped spring onions (scallions) to the sauce when frying the vegetables.

Measure the rice in a jug and note the volume. Place in a saucepan. Measure double the volume of boiling water and pour on to the rice. Add salt, cover, bring to the boil and simmer until all the water is absorbed and the rice is cooked.

Meanwhile, mix together the flours and egg white in a bowl with ½ tsp salt. Stir in 4-5 tbsp cold water to make a batter.

For the sauce, heat the groundnut (peanut) oil in a wok and fry the onion for around 5 minutes over a medium heat until it starts to turn golden. Add the (bell) peppers and carrot and continue to cook for a few minutes to soften.

Heat the vegetable oil in a large pan until a crumb of bread sizzles madly. Drop five or six pieces of pork in the batter, lift them out and allow excess batter to fall away. Fry them in the hot oil for 1½ minutes, until golden and cooked, lifting them out with a slotted spoon and on to a plate lined with kitchen paper. Cook all the pork like this.

Return to the sauce. Stir together the ketchup, vinegar, soy sauce, sugar and cornflour (cornstarch). Add to the pan of stir-fried vegetables with the pineapple and juice. Season. Bring everything up to a simmer, then drop the pork into it. Toss to warm through, then serve with the rice.

Our favourite pasta carbonara

This is my standby supper dish when there's nothing in but the basics. Even the most limp bit of parsley comes to life when tossed together with the other ingredients. The secret to a really good carbonara, though, is to make sure everything is ready at the point when you drain the spaghetti. The pasta needs to be really hot when you add the egg mixture so the egg cooks just enough to make a sauce, but not to scramble it.

Prep: 15 minutes
Cook: 20 minutes
Serves 4

4 streaky bacon rashers (strips), chopped
½ onion, finely chopped
400g/14oz spaghetti or linguine
Salt and freshly ground black pepper
4 medium eggs
50g/1¾oz Parmesan, grated,
   plus extra to serve
A handful of fresh parsley, chopped

clever cooking

~ I've found the cooking time of different dried pastas vary a bit, so I always start to test it about 1-2 minutes before the time stated on the pack.

~ If you're using streaky bacon that's had the fat cut off, you may need a drizzle of oil to help it cook. Take care not to add too much, though, otherwise the finished dish will taste greasy rather than creamy –1 tsp olive oil should do it.

Put the bacon and onion in a frying pan (skillet) and place over a medium heat. Season well. (There's no need to add any oil – the fat from the bacon will be enough.) Cook until the bacon is crispy.

Meanwhile, boil the pasta in a large pan of salted water just until al dente.

Mix the eggs, Parmesan and parsley together in a bowl and season with black pepper – there'll be enough salt in there from the cheese.

Drain the pasta, leaving a little cooking water clinging to it. Tip back into the pan. Add the bacon and onion and the egg mixture. Stir very quickly, then divide between four bowls. Serve with extra grated Parmesan.

Real burgers

This is a cinch to put together and takes hardly any time to make. If you have a good butcher, ask for very lean minced (ground) beef. You need to get everything ready to go so that once the burgers are cooked they can be served straightaway. When homemade chips seem a stretch too far, we do a run to the local chip shop.

Prep: 20 minutes
Cook: 15 minutes
Serves 4

Iceberg lettuce
500g/1lb 2oz good-quality minced (ground)
    beef
A handful of fresh parsley, finely chopped
Salt and freshly ground black pepper
4 burger buns (or homemade rolls,
    see page 222)
2 beefsteak tomatoes, sliced
¼ red onion, sliced
Gherkins, either cocktail or large, sliced or
    chopped
Mayonnaise, ketchup and mustard, to serve

Also try this...

~ To my shame we have a slice of Dairylea on top. When the burger is nearly cooked, put a slice on each one. They'll melt quickly.

Pull off a couple of slices of lettuce for each burger.

Put the beef in a bowl, add the parsley and season well. Use a fork to break up the strands and mix everything together. Divide roughly into four. Shape each quarter into a burger measuring around 7cm/2¾in wide.

Heat a frying pan (skillet) until hot and add the burgers. Cook over a medium heat for 6-7 minutes – there's no need to move them around, just let them brown in the pan. Turn over and continue to fry for 6-7 minutes, until completely cooked. Put on a plate to rest for a couple of minutes.

Drain off the fat from the pan, leaving the juices in there. Put the base of the buns in the pan to toast and soak up the juices.

Divide the bases between four plates and top with a burger, putting some of the tomatoes, onion, gherkins and lettuce on each, and finish with the top of the burger bun. Let everyone help themselves to mayo, ketchup or mustard.

My mum's stew

This is an all-time family favourite. Although browning the beef takes a little time, once everything is in the pan and simmering away, the heat does all the work. It's a two-in-one treat, as the recipe can also be used to make a pastry-topped pie.

Prep: 30 minutes
Cook: 2 hours
Serves 4

15g/½oz beef dripping
500g/1lb 2oz braising beef
1 onion, roughly chopped
1 carrot, roughly chopped
1 turnip, roughly chopped
1 bay leaf
A few sprigs of fresh thyme
2 sprigs of fresh marjoram
150ml/5fl oz/⅔ cup beer
900ml/1½pt/4 cups hot beef stock
Salt and freshly ground black pepper

For the dumplings
100g/3½oz/scant ¾ cup self-raising flour
50g/1¾oz suet (shredded beef fat),
   or use lard

Melt the dripping in a pan over a medium heat and brown the beef in batches, taking care to get a nice bit of colour on each side. This takes a while, but it's worth it for the depth of flavour in the finished stew. Keep the heat at medium and take care that the fat doesn't burn in the bottom of the pan. Set the beef aside on a plate.

Add the vegetables to the pan and cook in the goodness at the bottom, stirring all the time, for about 5 minutes. You might need to add extra fat.

Return the beef to the pan and add the herbs, beer and stock. Season well. Cover, bring to the boil and simmer on a low heat on the hob for 1½ hours, until the beef is tender. It's ready when you can easily pull a piece apart.

Towards the end of the cooking time, make the dumplings. Sift the flour into a bowl and stir in the suet. Season, then drizzle a little water over the top. Stir with a fork and keep on drizzling the water in until you get a sticky dough. You should be able to handle it.

Increase the heat under the stew until it's bubbling hot and drop in 8 spoonfuls of the dumpling mixture, the size of an egg. Cover the pan and cook the dumplings for 10-12 minutes. Divide the stew between four plates, giving two dumplings each.

A beautiful Bolognese

Rich and savoury, with nuances of wine and herbs, this is a winner every time. Leaving it to simmer on the hob slowly tenderizes the meat and lends the dish a heartiness that's hard to beat. The liver gives it extra depth of flavour (without being offaly) and the splash of cream is a sublime flourish that rounds the sauce off perfectly.

Prep: 30 minutes
Cook: 1 hour 30 minutes
Serves 8 (see freezing tip, below)

25g/1oz/¼ stick butter
½ tbsp olive oil
2 bacon rashers (strips), chopped
1 onion, finely chopped
1 celery stick, chopped small
1 carrot, chopped small
1 garlic clove, minced
Salt and freshly ground black pepper
500g/1lb 2oz minced (ground) beef
100g/3½oz chicken livers, finely chopped
2 sprigs of fresh thyme and 1 bay leaf
400g/14oz canned chopped tomatoes
1 tbsp tomato purée (paste)
A splash of white or red wine
400ml/14fl oz/1¾ cups beef stock
4 tbsp double (heavy) cream
400g/14oz penne (enough for four)
Parmesan, grated, to serve
A handful of fresh parsley, chopped, to serve

To freeze
~ This makes enough sauce for eight servings. Spoon the remainder into a plastic container and cool. Cover and freeze for up to three months. Thaw overnight and use as above.

Melt the butter in a pan with the oil, then fry the bacon, onion, celery and carrot over a medium heat for 8-10 minutes, until softened. Stir in the garlic and cook for 1 minute. Season well.

Spoon on to a plate and set aside. Return the pan to the heat and add the beef. Use the back of a spoon to squash it down in the pan and brown well. Turn over and brown the other side. Chop it up with the spoon.

Stir in the chicken livers and return the vegetable mixture to the pan. Add the thyme, bay, tomatoes and tomato purée (paste). Give it a good stir, then add the wine and stock. Season well. Cover, bring to the boil, then simmer over a low heat for 1 hour. (Sometimes, if I fancy a smoother sauce, I take the stick blender round the pan for about 5 seconds.) Stir in the cream.

Towards the end of the cooking time, bring a large pan of salted water to the boil. Stir in the penne and cook according to the timing on the pack. Add a spoonful of cooking water to the sauce, then drain the pasta. Return it to the pan and stir in half the sauce (see tip left). Divide between four bowls and serve sprinkled with some grated Parmesan and chopped parsley.

The broth and boiled beef I grew up on

Mum, at 90, still makes Scotch broth every week (remember, Highland summers are short!). The primary school was yards from our house and my sisters and I used to come home for lunch. On soup day there was always a race to be the first to scoop out the marrow from the bone. The broth serves four on two consecutive days. The 'second day' broth is even better once the barley has plumped up and the overall dish is denser.

Prep: 15 minutes
Cook: 2 hours 20 minutes
Serves 4-8

1 piece of marrow bone from the butcher
1.4kg/3lb piece beef skirt or runner
   (skirt steak)
300g/10½oz soup or broth mix
2 medium carrots, finely chopped
1 parsnip, finely chopped
2 medium onions, finely chopped
¼ white cabbage, finely chopped
1 leek, finely chopped
A handful of fresh parsley, roughly
   chopped, to serve

Put the bone and beef into a large stockpot and add 2.5ltr/4½pt/5½pt water to cover the meat. Bring to the boil; a layer of scum will form on the surface – just remove it with a large metal spoon or ladle and throw away.

Turn the heat down, add the soup or broth mix and simmer, partly covered, for 90 minutes. Check the pot from time to time and if more scum has formed, just skim it off. Add the chopped vegetables and a further 600ml/1pt/2½ cups water, bring to the boil and simmer for another 30 minutes.

Remove the bone and beef. Season the broth well and serve it sprinkled with chopped parsley. Slice the beef and serve after the soup, in the same soup plates, with mash and hot English mustard.

To freeze

~ If you'd rather not have the soup on two consecutive days, it freezes brilliantly.

Also try this...

~ If you don't want to include the meat, all is well – just add one or two meat stock cubes to the pan instead. It'll still be delicious.

Make one, freeze one lasagne

A fair amount of work goes into lasagne, so I make double and freeze half. If you have loads of time it's nice to make fresh pasta, but for ease this recipe uses ready-made.

Prep: 1 hour
Cook: 2 hours
Makes 2 lasagne, each to serve 4

25g/1oz/¼ stick butter
½ tbsp olive oil
4 bacon rashers (strips), chopped
1 onion, finely chopped
1 celery stick, finely chopped
1 carrot, finely chopped
Salt and freshly ground black pepper
1 garlic clove, crushed
700g/1lb 9oz minced (ground) beef
2 sprigs of fresh thyme
1 bay leaf
400g/14oz canned chopped tomatoes
1 tbsp tomato purée (paste)
A splash of white or red wine
500ml/18fl oz/2¼ cups beef stock
20 no-cook lasagne sheets
24 fresh basil leaves
75g/2¾oz Parmesan, grated

For the white sauce
100g/3½oz/scant 1 stick butter
100g/3½oz/scant ¾ cup plain
  (all-purpose) flour
1.4ltr/2½pt/6¼ cups milk
Freshly grated nutmeg

To freeze
~ Cover the uncooked lasagne with clingfilm (plastic wrap) and freeze for up to three months. Thaw overnight, then cook as per the recipe.

Melt the butter in a large pan with the oil, then fry the bacon, onion, celery and carrot over a medium heat for 8-10 minutes, until softened, seasoning well. Stir in the garlic and cook for 1 minute. Spoon on to a plate.

Return the pan to the heat and brown the beef. Turn over and brown the other side, then chop with the spoon.

Slide the veg back into the pan and add the thyme, bay, tomatoes and purée (paste). Stir, then pour in the wine and stock. Season, cover and bring to the boil. Reduce the heat and simmer for 1 hour.

For the white sauce, put the butter, flour and 1.2ltr/2pt/5 cups of the milk in a large pan and heat slowly, whisking. Simmer for 5 minutes, until it's thickened. Season well and grate in a little nutmeg.

Preheat the oven to 200°C/180°C fan/400°F/gas mark 6. Put a little beef in two 1.2ltr/2pt/2½pt oven- and freezer-proof dishes. Lay a few basil leaves on top. Cover with two pasta sheets. Spoon white sauce over each, then add a little Parmesan. Layer each dish up until you've used all the ingredients. Stir the remaining milk into the last portion of white sauce to loosen it. The top layers should be pasta, then white sauce and Parmesan. Set one dish aside to cool (see tip). Bake the other dish for 30-40 minutes, until golden and bubbling.

Food for the kids' mates

Food for the kids' mates

Instant fresh pesto with pasta

My friend Jeff showed me that you don't need many basil leaves to make a good pesto – in fact just 16! I make this in a food processor, which chops the basil and nuts finely, then mix with the Parmesan at the end to give the sauce some texture.

Prep: 10 minutes
Cook: 10 minutes
Serves 4

400g/14oz dried linguine
16 fresh basil leaves
25g/1oz pine nuts
½ garlic clove
100ml/3½fl oz/scant ½ cup olive oil
50g/1¾oz Parmesan, grated,
   plus extra to serve
Salt and freshly ground black pepper

Bring a large pan of salted water to the boil and cook the pasta according to the timings on the pack.

Meanwhile put the basil, pine nuts and garlic in a food processor. Whiz to chop the ingredients roughly. With the motor running, slowly pour in the oil to make a thick sauce. Spoon into a bowl and stir in the Parmesan, then season to taste.

Drain the pasta, leaving a little water behind to cling to it. Stir in the pesto, then divide between four bowls. Offer extra Parmesan to anyone who'd like more.

To freeze

~ Put in a sealable container and cover with a little olive oil – the pesto will be fine stored in the fridge for up to five days. Or freeze for up to a month in an airtight container. Thaw overnight to use.

Also try this...

~ Although it's traditionally served with pasta, a spoonful of pesto drizzled over a steak, tossed through roasted vegetables or over the Woodfired pizzas on page 100 is lovely.

~ I sometimes use this energy-saving method to cook the pasta: add the pasta to a pan of boiling salted water and cover. Bring back to the boil, then turn off the heat, leaving the lid on and allow it to 'cook' in the water for the time stated on the pack.

~ If you've got extra time, toast the pine nuts until golden for a deeper flavour.

Fried cheesy sandwich

I picked up this recipe from my friend, the food and wine writer Richard Erlich. It's great to do for just one person, which I've given instructions for here, and can be multiplied up easily. Buttering the outside may seem like a naughty treat, but the fact is you'd be buttering the inside anyway and it completely transforms a humble sandwich into an indulgent snack.

Prep: 5 minutes
Cook: 5 minutes
Serves 1

A little softened butter
2 slices of stale bread
1 slice of ham
Cheddar cheese
A little chutney

Butter one side only of each slice of bread, then lay them buttered side down on a board. Put the ham on one slice, then grate enough cheese to cover it. Spread the other slice with chutney and place on top of the cheese slice.

Heat a frying pan (skillet) until hot – there's no need for any oil here. Slide the sandwich into the pan and cook for 1-2 minutes, until golden, then turn over and cook for another minute. The inside will be meltingly gorgeous.

Clever cooking

~ If you're making more than one sandwich, ensure the pan doesn't get too hot by moderating the heat. You don't want it to be smoking, or else the butter and sandwich will burn easily and ruin the overall flavour.

The ultimate veggie curry

The combination of butter-soft aubergine, nutty chickpeas and hit of chilli-hot spice makes this one of my all-time favourites. A generous handful of coriander (cilantro) and lots of plain yogurt served alongside is a must – the cool tanginess providing the perfect counterbalance to the warm spices.

Prep: 30 minutes
Cook: 40 minutes
Serves 4

3 tbsp vegetable oil
1 onion, finely sliced
2 garlic cloves, sliced
A small chunk of fresh root ginger, peeled and chopped
1 tsp ground cumin
Seeds from 2 cardamom pods, ground
1 tsp ground coriander
½ tsp chilli powder
¼ tsp turmeric
½ aubergine (eggplant), roughly chopped
350g/12oz potatoes, chopped into 2.5cm/1in dice
2 plum tomatoes, roughly chopped
1 tbsp tomato purée (paste)
500ml/18fl oz/2¼ cups hot vegetable stock
A handful of green beans, halved
400g/14oz canned chickpeas (garbanzo beans), drained
Salt and freshly ground black pepper

To serve
Flatbreads or naan
Plain yogurt
Fresh coriander (cilantro)

Heat 2 tbsp of the oil in a medium-sized pan and cook the onion over a fairly high heat for 8-10 minutes, until golden round the edges. Stir in the garlic, ginger and spices. Continue to cook for 2-3 minutes, adding a little boiling water now and then, stirring all the time and simmering the mixture until the spices and onions take on a sauciness.

Add the remaining 1 tbsp oil, the aubergine (eggplant) and potatoes and cook in the sauce for a further 5 minutes until everything is coated in the spice mix and it is starting to cook and turn golden.

Stir in the tomatoes, tomato purée (paste), stock, green beans and chickpeas (garbanzo beans) and season well. Cover and bring to the boil, then reduce the heat and simmer for 15-20 minutes until the potatoes are tender.

Spoon into bowls and serve with flatbreads or naan, lots of cooling yogurt and fresh coriander (cilantro).

More people to feed?

~ To stretch this to feed more, serve with basmati rice (50g/1¾oz per person).

Tear-and-share cheesy rolls

I'm a bit of a baking fanatic and particularly love making bread. These rolls are dead easy to do and look impressive, yet they are a fraction of the price of shop-bought ones. The dough is enriched with butter and egg, which makes the rolls deliciously soft.

Prep: 15 minutes,
   plus 1 hour rising and proving
Cook: 30-35 minutes
Makes 8 rolls

700g/1lb 9oz/5 cups strong white bread flour
3-4 sprigs of fresh thyme, plus extra for
   the top
10g/¼oz fast-action dried (active dry) yeast
1½ tsp salt
100g/3½oz Cheddar cheese, grated
50g/1¾oz/scant ½ stick butter, chopped
1 medium egg, beaten

Put the flour in a large bowl or the bowl of a free-standing mixer. Pull the leaves off the thyme and add to the flour. Stir in the yeast, salt and half the cheese.

Measure 350ml/12fl oz/1½ cups hot water in a jug. Add the butter and stir to melt it.

If making the dough by hand, form a well in the centre and pour in the liquid. Add the egg and stir with a knife to mix everything together to make a rough dough. Tip on to a board and knead for a good 10 minutes until smooth and sticky. Resist adding any more flour, as it will make the finished loaf dry. (If doing this bit in a mixer, pour in the liquid and egg and mix together with a dough hook.)

Cover the bowl and leave in a warm place for 30-40 minutes, until the dough springs back when you press it.

Scrape the dough out of the bowl and cut it into eight rough pieces. Quickly shape into rolls, without knocking out too much air.

Put on a baking sheet lined with baking parchment, with one roll in the middle and the others loosely around it in a flower shape. Each roll will expand into the next one. Cover and put in a warm place for 30 minutes.

Meanwhile, preheat the oven to 190°C/ 170°C fan/375°F/gas mark 5. Sprinkle the remaining cheese and extra thyme leaves over the rolls and bake in the oven for 30-35 minutes, until evenly golden all over and the rolls sound hollow when tapped on top.

Cool on a wire rack, then move on to a board and let everyone tear off their own roll.

Clever cooking

~ You can sometimes buy fresh yeast from behind the bakery counter in the supermarkets and in health-food shops. You'll need 20g for this recipe. To use, dissolve in a little of the water first, then add along with the other ingredients.

~ The amount of liquid needed will vary, depending on how fresh the flour is. Don't worry if you think you've added too much; it's better to have a slightly wetter dough than a dry one.

~ I've made the rolls quite chunky, but the dough could easily split into 12 smaller rolls, if you prefer.

To freeze

~ Freeze leftover rolls, wrapped tightly in clingfilm (plastic wrap), for a month. Thaw for a couple of hours, then warm through in the oven.

Baked chicken casserole

This complete meal is something I make most weeks when I need to see off those lonesome bits at the bottom of the fridge – the half red pepper, yellowing leek, slightly bendy carrot. I draw the line at yellowing broccoli, though. The balsamic (my son Ewan's suggestion) gives extra depth and a little sweetness to the dish.

Prep: 15 minutes
Cook: 1¼ hours
Serves 4

Olive oil
A large knob (pat) of butter
1 whole small chicken, jointed,
    or 8 thighs (skin on)
Whatever the veg drawer offers –
    a leek, a carrot, ½ aubergine
    (eggplant), ¼ squash, a couple
    of potatoes and an onion
½ lemon
A few garlic cloves
A few fresh herbs, such as
    rosemary, marjoram or thyme
600ml/1pt/2½ cups hot chicken stock
    (a cube is fine)
Salt and freshly ground black
    pepper
A good drizzle of balsamic vinegar

1

1. Preheat the oven to 180°C/160°C fan/350°F/ gas mark 4. Place a large flameproof and ovenproof roasting tin on the hob and heat 2 tbsp oil and the butter. Brown the chicken in this, turning every 2 minutes.

2-3. Chop the vegetables into bite-size pieces.

4. Add the veg to the pan.

2

3

4

Also try this...

~ If you have any dregs of wine hanging about, tip into the pan and let it evaporate a little before adding the stock.

5. Squeeze over the lemon and put the squeezed half in the pan with the garlic and herbs. Toss to coat everything in the oil.

6-7. Finally add the stock and a little seasoning. Throw over some balsamic vinegar and an extra drizzle of olive oil.

8. Bake in the oven for about 1¼ hours, until the chicken is cooked through, turning everything over a couple of times during the cooking.

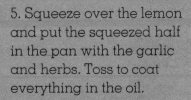

5

6

7

8

Rory's chicken burritos with flatbreads

This is a dish that my son Rory likes me to do when he has his college mates back and they're all hungry. It's great to cook for a crowd as you can spread out the dishes and let everyone make their own parcels with as much or as little from each bit as they like.

Prep: 40 minutes
Cook: 40 minutes
Serves 4

For the flatbreads
300g/10½oz/generous 2 cups strong
   white bread flour, plus extra for dusting
1 tsp fast-action dried (active dry) yeast
½ tsp salt
2 tsp olive oil

For the marinated chicken
3 chicken breasts, skinless and boneless
Olive oil
A little unwaxed lemon zest
A squeeze of lemon
1 sprig of fresh rosemary, roughly chopped
2 sprigs of fresh thyme, roughly chopped
Salt and freshly ground black pepper

For the salsa
200g/7oz cherry tomatoes, roughly chopped
¼ red onion, very finely chopped
A squeeze of lime
1 red chilli pepper, halved, de-seeded
   and finely chopped
A small handful of fresh coriander
   (cilantro) leaves
1 tsp olive oil

For the guacamole
1 avocado, halved and pitted
¼ red onion, very finely chopped
A squeeze of lime

For the beans
A knob (pat) of butter
1 garlic clove, crushed
400g/14oz canned black beans,
   drained and rinsed

To serve
125g/4½oz/generous ½ cup long-grain rice
Grated Cheddar cheese
Soured cream
Lime wedges

Clever cooking
~ Some canned beans have salt or sugar added. If you buy beans in water only, there's no need to rinse them. Just drain in a colander and shake.

More people to feed?
~ This could serve six to eight if you make more dough and cut the chicken into narrower pieces. Thin the soured cream down with a splash of milk or water and grate more cheese. To make six flatbreads use 450g/1lb/3¼ cups flour, 1½ tsp yeast, ¾ tsp salt and 1 tbsp olive oil. For eight, double the quantities above.

Make the dough for the flatbreads. Sift the flour into a large bowl and then stir in the yeast and salt. Make a well in the centre, then add the olive oil and 200ml/ 7fl oz/scant 1 cup lukewarm water. Mix with a knife to get all the ingredients together, then tip on to a board and knead until soft and sticky – about 10 minutes. Return to the bowl and set aside for at least 20 minutes. (You can also do this with a free-standing mixer and dough hook; just leave the dough in the bowl.)

Marinate the chicken. Line a large board with clingfilm (plastic wrap), then place the chicken breasts on top of it, each breast a little bit apart. Cover with another sheet of clingfilm (plastic wrap). Take a rolling pin and bash each piece until it's a thin flat shape. Uncover and put the pieces in a large flat dish. Drizzle with a little olive oil, then add the lemon zest, juice and herbs. Season well and turn each piece of meat over to coat in the marinade. Cover and chill.

Make the salsa. Put all the ingredients in a bowl and season well. At the same time, put the Cheddar in a separate bowl, the soured cream in another bowl and the lime wedges in another.

Measure the rice in a jug and note the volume. Put into a pan and add double the volume of boiling water. Add salt, cover, bring to the boil and turn the heat down to its lowest setting. Cook until all the water is absorbed.

Make the guacamole. Spoon the avocado into a bowl and roughly crush with a fork. Add the red onion and mix together until mushy. Season with the lime juice and salt and pepper.

For the beans, melt the butter in a pan and fry the garlic for 1 minute. Add the beans and a splash of water. Season and heat through. Mash well. Spoon into a bowl.

Heat a frying pan (skillet) or griddle (grill pan) to medium-hot and cook the chicken for 5 minutes. Turn over when the chicken has almost cooked on top and it looks just a bit pink and fleshy still, then cook for a further 3 minutes, until cooked through. Set aside on a plate.

Heat a separate large flat frying pan (skillet) for the flatbreads. Tip the dough on to a floured board – it'll be quite sticky – then cut it into four pieces. Roll one out to a thin round shape and place in the hot frying pan to cook while you roll out the next. It's ready to turn when lots of bubbles appear on top. This takes just a minute or two. Turn over and cook briefly until the bubbly bits are just golden on the other side. Put on a plate. Repeat to make all four flatbreads.

Cut the chicken into thick slices, then put all of the components on the table and everyone can get stuck in. You put whatever you fancy in the centre of the flatbread, and wrap it up like a parcel.

My take on chicken twizzlers

Kids love these tasty morsels, and they contain nothing scary. A little goes a long way: three good-sized chicken breasts is plenty for four people. The seasoning is subtle here – mustard provides a mellowness, while the paprika lends a hint of smokiness. Serve with a tiny sprinkle of salt and tomato ketchup for dipping.

Prep: 20 minutes
Cook: 25 minutes
Serves 4

6 slices of white bread, crusts removed
2 tbsp roughly chopped fresh parsley
5 tbsp plain (all-purpose) flour
1½ tsp English mustard powder
½ tsp smoked sweet paprika
Salt and freshly ground black pepper
3 medium eggs
3 chicken breasts (around 500g/1lb 2oz
    total weight), skinless and boneless,
    cut into finger-width slices
Vegetable oil, for shallow-frying
Tomato ketchup, to serve

Break the bread into pieces and whiz in a food processor to make breadcrumbs. Tip into a large shallow dish and then stir in the parsley.

Put the flour in a separate shallow dish and stir in the mustard and paprika. Season well. Crack the eggs into another shallow dish and beat together.

Dip each chicken slice into the flour mixture to coat, then into the egg, then into the breadcrumbs.

Heat a little oil in a frying pan (skillet) and fry the chicken in five or six batches over a medium heat for a couple of minutes on each side, until nicely golden and cooked in the middle. They're ready when they feel firm when pressed with a knife. To check the thicker pieces are cooked, cut through the middle.

Divide between four plates. Sprinkle with salt and serve with tomato ketchup.

clever cooking

~ If you'd prefer to cook these in the oven, spread them out on two baking sheets lined with baking parchment. Drizzle with a little olive oil and bake for around 20 minutes at 200°C/180°C fan/400°F/ gas mark 6.

Clissold fried chicken

My version of KFC (we live near Clissold Park in north London). Although not the healthiest of dishes, at least you can buy good-quality meat and know exactly what goes into it. Serve with a big salad on the side and lots of paper napkins!

**Prep: 15 minutes, plus at least
  2 hours to marinate**
Cook: 30 minutes
Serves 4

2 tbsp white wine vinegar
3 tbsp chicken seasoning
3 garlic cloves, crushed
2 tbsp roughly chopped fresh parsley
8 chicken drumsticks, skin removed
3 tbsp plain (all-purpose) flour
2ltr/3½pt/8 cups vegetable or
  sunflower oil, for frying

Put the vinegar, 2 tbsp of the chicken seasoning, the garlic and parsley in a sealable container. Add the drumsticks and toss to coat, then cover and chill for at least 2 hours.

When ready to cook, preheat the oven to 200°C/180°C fan/400°F/gas mark 6.

Put the flour into a shallow bowl and add the remaining 1 tbsp chicken seasoning. Roll the chicken in this.

Heat the vegetable oil in a large pan until a crumb of bread sizzles madly. Deep-fry the drumsticks in batches until golden. Lift out on to a roasting tin, then finish off cooking in the oven – they'll take around 20 minutes, but have a good poke with a sharp knife to check there's no bloodiness before serving.

Save money

~ This is a great one to do if there's an offer on mixed packs of chicken drumsticks and thighs. Just skin the thighs first, then prepare and cook as above.

Watch your weight

~ Reduce the fat and calories of this by shallow-frying the chicken instead. Heat 1cm/½in vegetable oil in a frying pan (skillet) until hot and cook the drumsticks for 1 minute on each side, until golden. Put in a roasting tin and continue to bake in the oven at 200°C/180°C fan/400°F/gas mark 6 for 25 minutes, until cooked all the way through. They'll have a softer texture but be no less delicious.

Easy Asian chicken with satay sauce and jasmine lemon rice

At first glance, this may look like an intricate recipe, but it isn't at all. The ingredients for the marinade take minutes to put together and the sauce is an all-in-one heat-up job. It's a good midweek recipe and the kids will love it for the fresh-tasting Asian-style flavours.

Prep: 15 minutes
Cook: 20 minutes
Serves 4

For the chicken
3 chicken breasts
   (around 500g/1lb 2oz total weight)
1 garlic clove, crushed
2.5cm/1in piece of fresh root ginger,
   peeled and grated
1 lemongrass stalk, finely chopped
1 tbsp vegetable oil
Juice of 1 lime
Salt and freshly ground black pepper

For the satay sauce
100g/3½oz crunchy peanut butter
100g/3½oz coconut cream
2 tbsp soy sauce
100ml/3½fl oz/scant ½ cup chicken
   or vegetable stock

For the rice
250g/9oz/1⅓ cup Thai jasmine rice
1 jasmine tea bag
Zest of ¼ unwaxed lemon

Soak 12 wooden skewers in water. Slice the chicken, across the grain, into finger-width pieces. Put it in a non-metallic dish. Add the garlic, ginger, lemongrass, oil and lime juice and season. Toss, cover and chill.

For the satay sauce, put everything in a pan. Bring to the boil and simmer for 2-3 minutes until thickened, stirring. It thickens as it cools and is best served warm.

Put the rice in a measuring jug, note the volume and pour into a pan. Measure double the volume of boiling water in a jug and make jasmine tea with the tea bag (remove the bag). Stir in the lemon zest. Pour over the rice, add a pinch of salt, then cover the pan and bring to the boil. Reduce the heat to its lowest setting and simmer for 10 minutes, or as instructed on the packet.

Preheat the grill (broiler) to medium hot. Thread two or three pieces of chicken on to each skewer. Grill (broil) the chicken for 12-15 minutes, turning halfway through. Cut through the thickest meat on one of the skewers to check it's done. If it's still pink, grill (broil) until cooked through.

Divide the rice between four plates and top with the skewers. Spoon the sauce into a bowl and let everyone help themselves.

Woodfired pizza and our favourite toppings

Making pizza from scratch is a cinch and cheaper than buying a takeaway. When the weather's fine, I have the woodfired oven on in the garden and cook it in there. Each takes 2 minutes. We all like different toppings, but be wary of overloading the pizza, or mixing too many flavours. My favourite is finely sliced onion, pine nuts and raisins. Rory likes mushrooms, so long as they're covered with cheese (or else they go dry) and Ewan has pepperoni.

Prep: 30 minutes
Cook: 20 minutes
Serves 4

200g/7oz/scant 1½ cups plain (all-purpose) flour
200g/7oz/scant 1½ cups strong white bread flour
7g/¼oz fast-action dried (active dry) yeast
1 tsp salt
1 tbsp olive oil

For the topping
200ml/7fl oz/scant cup tomato passata (strained tomatoes)
1 garlic clove, sliced
Olive oil
A selection of yummy bits to go on top, such as sliced chestnut (cremini) mushrooms, finely sliced onion, pine nuts, raisins, sliced Italian pepperoni, anchovies, capers, black olives (pitted)
250g/9oz mozzarella cheese, thinly sliced
Salt and freshly ground black pepper

Also try this...

~ To flavour the passata sauce, chop a few herbs - whatever you have to hand - and stir them in. Alternatively use a few basil leaves, no matter how limp; just whip them out before you start ladling the sauce over the pizza dough.

To freeze

~ The sauce takes only minutes to make, but I always do double and freeze it for next time.

1. Preheat your normal, indoor oven to its highest setting. Place two heavy-based baking sheets in there on separate shelves to heat up. Sift the flours into a large bowl and stir in the yeast and salt. Make a well in the centre and add the olive oil and 250ml/9fl oz/generous cup lukewarm water. Stir with a knife, then tip on to a board and knead until smooth. (Or use a free-standing mixer.) Set aside for a minute.

2-4. Put the tomato passata (strained tomatoes) into a small pan. Add the garlic and a drizzle of olive oil. Bring to a simmer. If you are using the conventional oven, put a piece of baking parchment the same size as your baking sheet on top of the board to help you transfer the pizza to the oven. Roll out half the dough on top of it to fit the baking sheet. Set aside and do the same with another piece of parchment and dough.

5-8. Spoon a ladleful of tomato sauce on top of each, then add your yummy bits and some mozzarella and season. Slide the baking parchment on to the hot baking sheets and bake in the oven for 10 minutes. Slide the pizzas on to a board, cut each in half. Serve.

5

6

7

8

Pork, chickpea and chorizo stew

This gutsy dish uses only one pan – great for cutting down on the washing up.

Prep: 15 minutes
Cook: 20-25 minutes
Serves 4

1 tbsp olive oil
1 red onion, thinly sliced
1 red (bell) pepper, sliced
1 garlic clove, sliced
400g/14oz pork tenderloin,
   cut into bite-sized pieces
8 mini cooking chorizo sausages
1 tsp smoked sweet paprika
400g/14oz canned chopped tomatoes
150ml/5fl oz/⅔ cup hot chicken
   or vegetable stock
Salt and freshly ground black pepper
400g/14oz canned chickpeas (garbanzo
   beans), drained and rinsed

Heat the oil in a large pan and add the onion and pepper. Cook over a medium heat for 5 minutes, until the onion starts to turn golden and the pepper softens. Stir in the garlic and cook for 1 minute.

Add the pork and chorizo and brown quickly. Stir in the paprika, then add the tomatoes and stock. Season well, cover and bring to the boil. Turn the heat down to a simmer and cook for 10 minutes, or until the pork is cooked.

Tip the chickpeas (garbanzo beans) into the pan and then cook for a further 2-3 minutes to heat through. Spoon into bowls and serve with crusty bread.

More people to feed?

~ This is another dish that gets better the day after you've made it. If you need to stretch it to feed six, stir in a couple of handfuls of spinach with the chickpeas at the end of cooking and serve with rice or couscous.

Also try this...

~ If you prefer to use chicken it works just as well.

Moussaka that's stood the test of time

I learned to make this recipe in the 1970s and have loved it ever since. It's rich, so a little goes a long way, and all it needs is a green salad to serve alongside it. I like the way the topping is refreshingly tangy from the yogurt, with just a touch of cheese.

Prep: 40 minutes
Cook: 1 hour
Serves 4

1 medium aubergine (eggplant)
Olive oil
400g/14oz minced (ground) lamb
1 onion, finely chopped
1 garlic clove, crushed
1 tsp paprika
1 sprig of fresh rosemary, finely chopped
400ml/14fl oz/1¾ cups hot lamb, chicken
   or vegetable stock
Salt and freshly ground black pepper
1 large tomato, sliced
150g/5½oz plain yogurt
2 large egg yolks
25g/1oz/1 tbsp plain (all-purpose) flour
50g/1¾oz mature Cheddar cheese, grated

Preheat the oven to 220°C/200°C fan/425°F/gas mark 7.

Slice the aubergine (eggplant) into rounds, each about 6mm/¼in thick, and brush both sides with oil. Place on a baking sheet lined with baking parchment and roast in the oven for 20 minutes. Turn over and continue to roast for another 10 minutes.

Heat a medium pan – there's no need for any oil here – and brown the lamb for a good 5-10 minutes, breaking it up with a wooden spoon once it's cooked well. Remove from the pan. Add the onion to the pan and cook in the fat for about 5 minutes. Add the garlic, paprika and rosemary and cook for 1 minute.

Return the lamb to the pan and add the hot stock. Season well. Cover, bring to the boil and simmer for about 20 minutes.

Once the aubergine (eggplant) is roasted, remove from the oven and reduce the temperature to 200°C/180°C fan/400°F/gas mark 6. Layer the aubergine (eggplant) and lamb mixture up in a 1.2ltr/2pt/2½pt ovenproof dish – there should be two layers of each – finishing with the lamb. Cover with the tomatoes. Beat together the yogurt, egg yolks, flour and half the cheese and season. Spoon the sauce over the tomatoes to cover, then sprinkle with the remaining Cheddar.

Bake for 30 minutes until golden and bubbling. Allow to stand for 5-10 minutes before tucking in.

Make in advance

~ You can make this up to a day ahead if you need to – just layer it up to the tomato, cover and chill. Take the dish out of the fridge half an hour before cooking and complete recipe.

Diner-style pulled pork with sweet potato wedges and mango salsa

Rory and Ewan love Bodean's, an American diner in Soho. Here's my interpretation of one of their favourite meals there.

Prep: 20-30 minutes
Cook: 5 hours
Serves 4, with leftovers

For the pork
900g/2lb pork shoulder, boned
4 garlic cloves, crushed
1 tsp each of salt and freshly ground
   black pepper
2 tsp paprika
2 tsp English mustard powder
½ tsp ground cloves
3 tbsp white wine vinegar
A couple of dashes of Worcestershire sauce
1 tbsp tomato purée (paste)
30g/1¼oz light muscovado (soft light brown)
   sugar

For the sweet potato wedges
1 tbsp olive oil
1kg/2¼lb sweet potatoes, cut into wedges

For the salsa
2 mangoes, pitted and finely diced
¼ red onion, finely chopped
½ fresh red chilli pepper, finely chopped
1 tbsp white wine vinegar
1 tsp light muscovado (soft light brown)
   sugar
Juice of 1 lime

To marinate the pork, put all the pork ingredients in a large airtight container. Toss to coat the pork. Cover and chill overnight to allow the marinade to penetrate the meat.

Preheat the oven to 150°C/130°C fan/300°F/ gas mark 2.

Take the meat out of the fridge around 30 minutes before you're going to cook it. Put it on a rack in a roasting tin. Pour in 600ml/1pt/2½ cups boiling water, then cover the whole tin tightly with foil. Roast in the oven for at least 5 hours. It's ready when the meat shreds easily with a fork.

One hour and 15 minutes before the pork is ready, brush the oil all over the potato wedges and season well. Cook in a roasting tin underneath the pork until tender.

Mix together all the ingredients for the salsa and season well.

Put the pork on a board and use two forks to shred the meat. Divide between four plates and serve with the sweet potato wedges and the salsa.

More people to feed?

~ There's enough pork here to serve six to eight people. To make the two side dishes stretch further, add a bowl of long-grain rice, forked through with a knob (pat) of butter and some roughly chopped fresh parsley.

Clever cooking

~ The pork is in the oven for a long time, so the marinade will cook and stick to the bottom of the roasting tin. To make cleaning easier, line it with baking parchment beforehand.

Yummy potato and ham gratin

I saw this recipe in an old French cookery book one Christmas, when I was looking for something to use up leftover ham. It also called for all the other goodies that I had in – a little bit of cream left in a carton, some cheese, and of course potatoes. It's delicious and warming for any time of year and would easily stretch to feed more as it's so rich.

Prep: 20 minutes
Cook: 45 minutes
Serves 4, with leftovers

A little butter, for greasing
2 shallots, finely chopped
1 garlic clove, crushed
4 large potatoes (around 1kg/2¼lb total
   weight), grated
100g/3½oz ham, roughly chopped
50g/1¾oz Cheddar cheese or
   Parmesan, grated
4 medium eggs, beaten
4 tbsp single (light) cream
A handful each of fresh parsley
   and chives, roughly chopped
Salt and freshly ground black pepper

Preheat the oven to 200°C/180°C fan/400°F/ gas mark 6. Butter a 2ltr/3½pt/good 2 quart ovenproof dish.

Put all the ingredients in a large bowl, season well and mix.

Spoon into the prepared dish and bake for around 45 minutes, until golden all over and the potato is cooked.

Allow to stand for 10 minutes before tucking in.

Also try this...

~ When this is cold, it tastes a little bit like a grated potato omelette. Serve in slices, warmed through in the oven if you like, with some bacon for breakfast.

~ If you don't eat it all, this will keep fine, covered in the fridge, for up to three days.

My mum's mince and tatties

This is a favourite in our house, particularly when I serve it with a generous dollop of creamy mashed potatoes (or 'tatties', as they are called in Scotland).

Prep: 10 minutes
Cook: 1¾ hours
Serves 4

500g/1lb 2oz fresh minced (ground) beef
Salt and freshly ground black pepper
1 medium onion, roughly chopped
2 chunky carrots, roughly chopped
1 small turnip, roughly chopped
600ml/1pt/2½ cups beef stock
1 tsp Bovril (yeast extract)

For the mash
900g/2lb potatoes, chopped into
   large chunks
100ml/3½fl oz/scant ½ cup milk
50g/1¾oz/scant ½ stick butter

Heat a saucepan until hot and add the beef, spreading it over the base of the pan. Season and brown over a medium heat. Resist turning the meat until it's lovely and brown, then allow it to cook on the other side. Lift out of the pan and put on a plate.

Add the onion, carrots and turnip to the pan, and cook for a minute or two in the pan juices. Return the mince to the pan and add the stock and Bovril (yeast extract). Cover and simmer for 1 hour.

While the beef is cooking, make the mash. Put the potatoes in a pan and cover with cold water. Add a pinch of salt, and cook until tender (about 20 minutes). Drain well, return to the pan and heat for a few moments to dry the potatoes. Add the milk and butter and mash well. Season.

Divide the mash between four plates and top with the beef. Dig in!

More people to feed?

~ Thicken the liquid and this dish will be much more substantial. Put 1 tsp cornflour (cornstarch) in a small pot and add a couple of tbsp of the hot liquid. Blend together, then pour back into the pan. Simmer for a couple of minutes to thicken the sauce.

To freeze

~ The mince can be frozen. Spoon it into a freezerproof container and cool. Freeze for up to 3 months. Thaw overnight and reheat in a pan until bubbling hot.

Rory's spicy chilli and rice

Using both fresh chilli and chilli powder gives this quite a kick. Rory always adds ground cumin and coriander, which give it a special warmth.

Prep: 15 minutes
Cook: 1¼ hours
Serves 4

500g/1lb 2oz fresh minced (ground) beef
1 onion, finely chopped
1 green (bell) pepper, de-seeded
   and chopped
1 garlic clove, chopped
½ fresh red chilli pepper, chopped
½ tsp hot chilli powder
1 tsp ground cumin
1 tsp ground coriander
400g/14oz canned chopped tomatoes
400ml/14fl oz/1¾ cups hot beef stock
Salt and freshly ground black pepper
400g/14oz canned red kidney
   beans, drained

To serve
250g/9oz/1⅓ cup long-grain rice
Plain yogurt
Lime wedges
Tabasco sauce

Heat a large pan until hot and add the beef. Use the back of a wooden spoon to spread it out over the pan and allow it to brown. Turn over and brown the other side, then chop with a wooden spoon to break up the bits. Lift it out of the pan and into a bowl. Set aside.

Add the onion, green pepper and garlic to the pan and cook for 5 minutes to brown in the pan juices. There's no need to add oil at this stage. Stir in the red chilli pepper, chilli powder, cumin and coriander.

Return the beef to the pan, then add the chopped tomatoes and stock. Season well. Cover, bring to the boil, then reduce the heat and simmer for 1 hour. Add the beans about 15 minutes before the chilli is ready.

Cook the rice: pour it into a large pan, add 600ml/1pt /2½ cups boiling water and some salt, then cover and bring to the boil. Reduce the heat and cook according to the timings on the pack. Fluff up with a fork.

Serve the chilli with the rice, a generous dollop of yogurt and a wedge of lime. Offer the bottle of Tabasco to anyone who likes it even hotter.

Clever cooking

~ I buy kidney beans canned in water only. There's no need to rinse them – just drain and pop in the pan. The natural juices will help to thicken the chilli right at the very end. Thin with a little water if you need to.

To freeze

~ Spoon the chilli into a freezerproof container and cool. Freeze for up to three months. Thaw overnight and reheat in a pan until bubbling hot.

Food on the run

Food on the run

A great veg dish for leftover cheese

This is the best recipe for using up the odd chunks of dry cheese in the fridge. Steaming the broccoli and cauliflower over a pan of boiling water keeps it lovely and tender, and doesn't make the cheese sauce watery. I always make white sauce the all-in-one way and whisk like crazy to make sure it's smooth.

Prep: 10 minutes
Cook: 20 minutes
Serves 4

1 small head of broccoli
1 small head of cauliflower, with the tender
   inner leaves only
40g/1½oz/scant ½ stick butter
2 heaped tbsp plain (all-purpose) flour
500-600ml/18-20fl oz/2¼-2½ cups milk
150g/5½oz leftover cheese, such as Cheddar,
   Gruyère and Parmesan, grated
1 tsp Dijon mustard
Freshly grated nutmeg
Salt and freshly ground black pepper
Crusty bread, to serve

Preheat the grill (broiler). Bring some water to the boil in a pan and place a steamer on top of it.

Cut the broccoli into medium-size florets and chop the stalk into bite-size chunks. Do the same with the cauliflower, reserving the inner leaves.

Arrange the cauliflower and broccoli florets in the steamer, stalk-side down, and tuck the chunks of stalk in between. Lay any leaves on top. Cover and steam over a medium heat for about 8 minutes, until the stalks are just tender.

Meanwhile put the butter, flour and milk in a pan and, whisking constantly, bring to the boil. Keep whisking until smooth. Simmer for 2 minutes to cook out the flour. Stir in two-thirds of the cheese and all of the mustard, add nutmeg to taste and then season.

Spoon the veg into a shallow ovenproof dish, tucking any leaves evenly alongside the pieces. Pour over the cheese sauce, sprinkle over the remaining cheese and grill (broil) until golden. Serve immediately with crusty bread.

Kerry's polenta with mushroom sauce

My big sis Kerry is a vegetarian, and since she made this for me I've been cooking it myself. Polenta is so quick to cook – the type I use is done in a minute and tastes amazing. If you're speedy with a chopping knife, this can be ready and on the table in 15 minutes.

Prep: 5 minutes
Cook: 10 minutes
Serves 4

For the mushrooms
A drizzle of olive oil
A knob of butter
1 garlic clove, sliced
400g/14oz mushrooms, such as chestnut
   (cremini) and field (portobello), halved
   or sliced
A few sprigs of fresh thyme
Salt and freshly ground black pepper
A dollop of crème fraîche

For the polenta
200g/7oz/1 cup 1-minute polenta (cornmeal)
75g/2¾oz/scant ¾ stick butter
75g/2¾oz/1 cup Parmesan, grated,
   plus extra to serve

Pour 1 ltr/1¾pt/4 cups water into a pan, cover and bring to the boil.

For the mushrooms, heat the oil and butter in a pan and add the garlic, mushrooms and thyme. Season well, then cover and cook for a few minutes, stirring every now and then. The mushrooms will soak up all the oil, then they'll release their own juices. Uncover the pan and stir in the crème fraîche, then leave the sauce to simmer gently.

Once the pan of water is boiling, pour in the polenta (cornmeal) slowly, beating all the time to ensure it absorbs all the water. Add the butter and Parmesan, season and stir in.

Spoon the polenta on to four plates, then top with the mushroom sauce. Grate over extra Parmesan to serve.

Also try this...

~ The mushroom sauce is also great served with tagliatelle pasta. For extra flavour, chop a couple of rashers of streaky bacon, then fry in a dry frying pan (skillet) first, before adding the oil and butter.

Ewan's chicken fried rice

Here's something my son Ewan became obsessed with from the takeaway round the corner. I wanted to show him how easy it was to make from scratch with some healthy bits thrown in.

Prep: 10 minutes
Cook: 15 minutes
Serves 4

225g/8oz/generous cup long-grain rice
Salt and freshly ground black pepper
2 tsp vegetable oil
1 tsp sesame oil
3 chicken breasts, skinless and boneless,
    cut into bite-sized chunks
1 bunch spring onions (scallions), roughly
    chopped
2.5cm/1in piece fresh root ginger, grated
1 garlic clove, sliced
1 fresh red chilli pepper, de-seeded and
    finely chopped
2 big spoonfuls frozen peas
2 medium eggs, beaten
Soy sauce, to serve

Save time

~ If you're cooking rice one night for another supper, cook double and make this the following night. Spread the rice out on a plate to cool in a few minutes, then put into a sealable container and chill immediately. Be sure to reheat it thoroughly.

Pour the rice into a measuring jug and note the volume. Put in a pan and add double the volume of boiling water to rice. Add a pinch of salt, cover with a lid, bring to the boil and cook according to the timings on the pack. Drain.

Heat the oils in a large wok and fry the chicken, turning, for 8-10 minutes until golden. It should be almost cooked. Season well.

Add the spring onions (scallions), ginger, garlic, chilli pepper and peas, and carry on cooking until the other bits in the pan have softened and started to brown too.

Add the cooked rice and toss everything together. Use a wooden spoon to push the mixture to one side and pour the beaten eggs on to the other side. Allow to cook for a few minutes in the heat, then use the spoon to break up and scramble the eggs. Stir everything together again and season. Make sure the rice is thoroughly reheated.

Spoon into bowls and serve immediately with soy sauce.

Restaurant-style creamy fish stew

When I visited my friend Eva, who lives in Stockholm, she made this on the Friday night. I couldn't believe she'd rustled up a bowl of such deliciousness so quickly at the end of a busy week, but when she told me the recipe I realized how easy it was.

Prep: 20 minutes
Cook: 15 minutes
Serves 4

1 tbsp sunflower oil
1 garlic clove, crushed
2 leeks, chopped
250ml/9fl oz/scant 1¼ cups dry white wine
3 tbsp oyster sauce
250ml/9fl oz/generous cup double (heavy) cream
100ml/3½fl oz/⅓-½ cup crème fraîche
A pinch of saffron strands
A sprig of fresh thyme
400g/14oz firm white fish, chopped
300g/10½oz salmon, chopped
150g/5½oz peeled raw prawns (shrimp), de-veined

Heat the oil in a large saucepan and sauté the garlic and leeks for around 5 minutes until the leeks are starting to turn golden. Add the white wine and bring to the boil. Simmer for a couple of minutes to cook off the alcohol.

Add the oyster sauce, 200ml/7fl oz/¾-1 cup water, the double (heavy) cream and crème fraîche. Stir in the saffron and thyme. Bring to the boil again.

Add the fish and prawns (shrimp), then simmer until the fish is opaque, about 8 minutes.

Spoon into bowls and serve immediately. with crusty bread.

watch your weight

~ If you're not keen on using so much cream and crème fraîche, halve the quantity and make it up with fish stock instead.

Stir-fry prawns with a spicy sauce

Although there's a little bit of chopping to do for this recipe, it's quick to cook. You need to fry the onion over a fairly high heat first to get the flavour, then add all the remaining veg. The prawns go in at the last minute, as they cook in an instant (and turn chewy and hard if they're overcooked).

Prep: 10 minutes
Cook: 15 minutes
Serves 4

1 tbsp vegetable oil
1 small onion, roughly chopped
1 red (bell) pepper, halved, de-seeded
   and cut into chunks
A handful of green beans, roughly
   chopped
½ head of broccoli, cut into florets
200g/7oz medium egg noodles or ribbon
   rice noodles
200g/7oz peeled raw prawns (shrimp),
   de-veined
Salt and freshly ground black pepper
A sprinkling of toasted sesame seeds

For the spicy sauce
Juice of 1 lime
2 tsp toasted sesame oil, plus extra
   to dress the noodles
1 tbsp soy sauce
1 tbsp grated fresh root ginger
1 fresh red chilli pepper, de-seeded
   and finely chopped
1 tsp runny honey or maple syrup

Heat the oil in a wok and fry the onion over a fairly high heat until golden. Add the pepper, beans and broccoli and continue to stir-fry, tossing the veg around the pan to cook until just tender.

Cook the noodles according to the instructions on the pack.

Make the sauce by whisking all the ingredients together in a bowl.

Add the prawns (shrimp) to the wok, then pour over the sauce and toss to coat everything in the sauce. It's ready when the prawns (shrimp) have turned pink. Season.

Divide the noodles between four bowls, and drizzle with a little sesame oil. Spoon over the prawns (shrimp) and veg and sprinkle with the sesame seeds.

Save time
~ Prepare for the next stir-fry: make double the quantity of the spicy sauce and refrigerate, covered, for up to five days.

Also try this...
~ If there are veggies in the family, use chopped cashews instead of prawns and add at the same time. 50g/1¾oz will be enough for four.

Shortcut Thai green chicken curry

I love those pots of Thai green curry paste you get in the supermarkets. They're packed with flavour and contain all the ingredients you would use if you were making it from scratch. I'd never be able to use up a pot within the sell-by time, so whenever I buy one I bag it up into little portions of clingfilm (plastic wrap). They all go into a plastic sealable container, which I put in the freezer. That way, the strong, spicy smell doesn't invade everything else. There's no need to thaw before use; just pop into the pan and heat gently to melt. I cook this curry the Thai way: you make a spicy coconut broth first, then add the fresh chicken and veg.

Prep: 10 minutes
Cook: 15 minutes
Serves 4

250g/9oz/1⅓ cups Thai jasmine rice
Salt
1 tsp groundnut (peanut) oil
1 tbsp ready-made Thai green curry paste
400ml/14fl oz/1¾ cups coconut milk
300ml/10fl oz/1¼ cups hot chicken stock
4 chicken thighs, skinless and boneless,
    cut into bite-size chunks
A handful of mangetout (snow peas)
    or sugar-snap peas, halved
1 red (bell) pepper, de-seeded
    and sliced
2 heads pak-choi (bok-choy),
    roughly chopped
A splash of Thai fish sauce, if you have it
Soy sauce, to season
Fresh Thai or regular basil
1 lime, cut into 4 wedges

Measure the rice in a jug and pour into a pan. Add double the volume of boiling water. Add a pinch of salt, cover, bring to the boil and simmer on the lowest setting for around 10 minutes, until all the water has been absorbed and the rice is fluffy.

Meanwhile, heat the oil in a pan and add the curry paste. Stir-fry until you can smell the gorgeous spicy chilli aroma. Add the coconut milk and stock and then bring to a simmer.

Add the chicken and simmer for 5 minutes, until cooked through. Throw in the mangetout and red (bell) pepper and cook for 2 minutes, then add the pak-choi (bok-choy) and stir in. It'll be cooked in about a minute (make sure the chicken is cooked through). Season with fish sauce, if using, and soy sauce.

Divide the rice between four bowls, ladle over the curry and pop a sprig of basil on top of each. Serve with a wedge of lime to squeeze over.

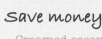

Save money

~ Creamed coconut, sold in little blocks, is a fraction of the price of coconut milk and keeps well in the fridge. Roughly chop 125g/4½oz and put in a bowl, then add 350ml/12fl oz/1½ cups boiling water. Stir to dissolve and it's ready to use.

~ This is a great one to do if you have leftover chicken from a roast. Just add it right at the end after cooking the veg to heat through.

~ This could easily stretch to feeding six if you needed to. Cook 400g/14oz/2 cups rice, then when you serve the curry, sprinkle over some chopped salted peanuts.

Crowd-pleasing pasta sauce

I got the idea for this Italian sauce when Matthew Drennan cooked it up in the Good Housekeeping Institute, London, while he was cookery editor there. I like to use Italian sausages, which have a much gutsier flavour. There's a little bit of cream added right at the end, but boy, does it taste so much richer for it.

Prep: 5 minutes
Cook: 20 minutes
Serves 4

400g/14oz pasta – conchiglie, tagliatelle and penne all work well
Salt and freshly ground black pepper
6 Italian-flavoured sausages
2 shallots, thinly sliced
200g/7oz canned chopped tomatoes
Finely grated zest of ½ unwaxed lemon
A pinch of dried chilli flakes
A pinch of sugar
200ml/7fl oz/¾-1 cup hot chicken stock
2 tbsp double (heavy) cream
A few fresh basil leaves, roughly torn, plus extra to garnish
Grated Parmesan, to serve

Bring a large pan of salted water to the boil and add the pasta. Cook, following the timings on the pack.

Put a large frying pan (skillet) over a medium heat. Skin the sausages and pop them in the pan with the shallots. (There's no need for any oil as the sausages contain enough fat.) Use a wooden spoon to start to break down the sausages and cook until golden. Season well.

Add the tomatoes, lemon zest, chilli, sugar and chicken stock. Simmer for 10 minutes, until the sausage is cooked through, then stir in the cream with the basil.

Drain the pasta, reserving a ladleful of the cooking water. Return the pasta and reserved water to the pan and add the sauce. Toss well and serve with grated Parmesan and a few basil leaves on top.

My Irish stew – in a dash

I bought my pressure cooker in a car boot sale about twenty years ago and it has become one of my most treasured pieces of kitchen kit. It's dead easy to use and cooks those warming stews we all crave in the winter in a fraction of the time. There's no need to brown anything off in this recipe, which saves even more time.

Prep: 10 minutes
Cook: 15 minutes
Serves 4

1 large onion, finely sliced
3 large carrots, sliced into chunks
4 potatoes (around 400g/14oz), peeled
   and quartered
2 lamb neck fillets (around 450g/1lb total
   weight), sliced into chunks
A handful of pearl barley
Salt and lots of freshly ground black pepper
500ml/18fl oz/2¼ cups hot lamb or
   chicken stock
A handful of chopped fresh parsley

Put the onion, carrots, potatoes, lamb and pearl barley into a pressure cooker. Season well. Pour over the stock.

Secure the lid and put the pan over a high heat. Bring up to pressure and cook for about 15 minutes. Release the pressure and open the lid.

Sprinkle the parsley over and serve.

Rory's quick steak with watercress and a hot horseradish dressing

This is one of those flash-in-the-pan suppers we love. My son Rory often cooks it as it's so quick to do and big on flavour. It's a great way of making a steak stretch further.

Prep: 5 minutes
Cook: 4-10 minutes
Serves 4

2 x 250-300g/9-10½oz rib-eye steaks
Vegetable or olive oil
Salt and freshly ground black pepper
150g/5½oz watercress
Crusty bread, to serve
Boiled new potatoes, tossed in butter,
   to serve

For the dressing
1 tbsp horseradish sauce
2 tbsp olive oil
1 tsp Dijon mustard
Juice of ½ lemon

Heat a dry frying pan (skillet) until hot. Brush the steaks with oil, then season and fry for 2-5 minutes on each side. The cooking time will depend on how thick the steaks are and how 'done' you like them. We like them medium-rare, so for a 2.5cm/1in thick steak, 2 minutes on each side is perfect. Put on a large plate and set aside to rest. (This allows all the juices to run through the meat and makes it more tender to slice.)

Put the watercress in a large shallow bowl. Beat together the horseradish, oil, mustard and lemon juice with about 1 tsp boiling water, to help the dressing come together.

Drizzle the dressing over the watercress and toss lightly. Slice the steak into fingers, then arrange on the watercress. Pop in the middle of the table and serve with crusty bread and a bowl of new potatoes tossed in butter.

Also try this...
~ Don't waste the pan juices! Pour any rested juices from the plate back into the frying pan (skillet). Add 2 tbsp boiling water and swirl the liquid around to mix with all the juices. Spoon over the steak just before serving it.

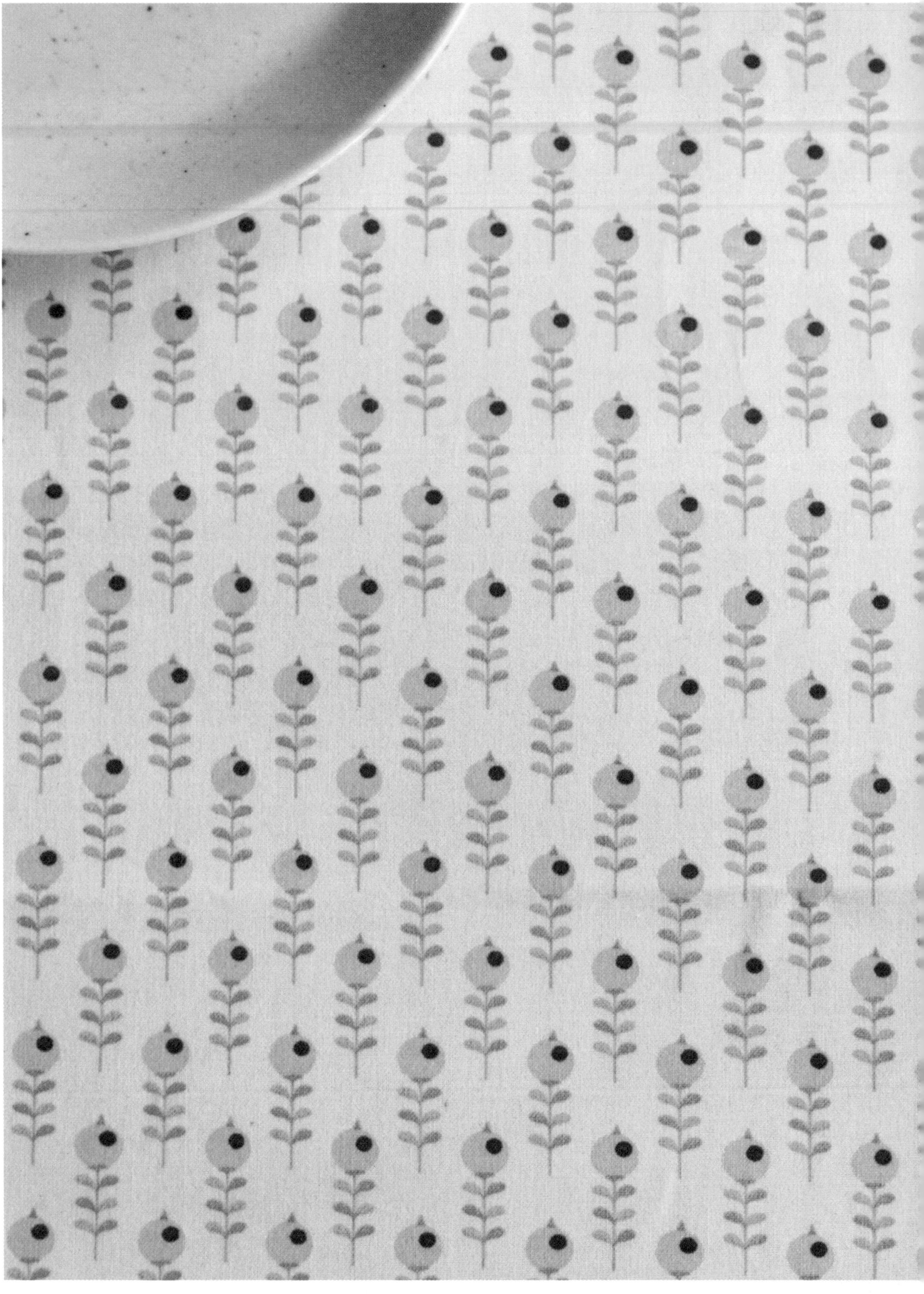

Weekend dinners

Weekend dinners

Onion bhajis

This is a lighter version of the cricket-ball-shaped onion bhaji many people are familiar with. There's no need to fry the onions first. All you do is marinate raw onions overnight in the spice mixture, then deep-fry until golden.

Prep: 20 minutes, plus overnight marinating
Cook: 20 minutes
Serves 4

2 medium onions, roughly sliced
1 small hot green chilli, chopped
A small handful of fresh coriander (cilantro) leaves, roughly chopped
2 tsp chilli powder
3 tsp cumin seeds
1 tsp turmeric
200g/7oz/scant 1½ cups gram (chickpea) flour
2 tsp salt, plus extra to sprinkle
Vegetable oil, for deep-frying

Put all the ingredients, except the oil, in a large sealable container and toss together well, making sure the onions are well coated in the floury mixture. Seal and chill overnight. (You need to leave them for this long to allow the mixture to draw the juices out of the onions and to form a sort of claggy batter around them.)

When ready to cook, heat the oil in a deep-fat fryer or large wok. The oil is ready when a breadcrumb dropped into it sizzles.

Drop spoonfuls of the mixture in batches into the hot oil and cook until golden. Lift out with a slotted spoon and drain on a plate lined with kitchen paper. Sprinkle with salt and then serve.

Love your leftovers

~ If you don't eat all the bhajis, put them in a sealable container and chill for up to two days. Reheat on a baking sheet for 2-3 minutes at 200°C/180°C fan/400°F/gas mark 6.

Dreamy-creamy fish pie

When I was growing up, the fish van used to come round on a Wednesday and my mum would make the most gorgeous fish pie in a huge Pyrex dish. It was very plain – haddock, parsley sauce and mashed potatoes. These days I like a little smoked fish in there to add flavour, and I think prawns make it more interesting. Tarragon (or dill) gives it a luxurious richness, as does the cream.

Prep: 30 minutes
Cook: 1 hour
Serves 4 generously

For the mash
1.2kg/2¾lb potatoes, quartered
A knob (pat) of butter, plus an extra knob,
  melted, to drizzle over
A splash of milk
Salt and freshly ground black pepper

For the filling
2 large eggs
25g/1oz/¼ stick butter, plus a little extra
35g/1½oz/2 tbsp plain (all-purpose) flour
500ml/18fl oz/2¼ cups milk
100ml/3½fl oz/scant ½ cup single (light)
  or double (heavy) cream
Leaves from either 2 sprigs of fresh tarragon
  or dill, roughly chopped
300g/10½oz haddock, cut into large chunks
100g/3½oz smoked haddock, cut into
  large chunks
200g/7oz raw shelled prawns (shrimp),
  de-veined

Put the potatoes in a large pan of boiling salted water. Cover and simmer for around 15 minutes, until tender. Drain well, add the butter and milk, season and mash well.

Hard-boil the eggs in a pan of boiling water for 8 minutes, then cool and shell them. Preheat the oven to 200°C/180°C fan/400°F/gas mark 6.

To make the white sauce, put the butter, flour and milk in a pan and whisk well. Bring up to the boil, whisking all the time, then cook for around 5 minutes until the mixture has thickened. Stir in the cream and your chosen herb, and season well.

Spoon all the fish and the prawns (shrimp) into a 2ltr/3½pt/good 2-quart ovenproof dish. Pour over the sauce to cover. Slice the eggs thinly and lay on top. Spoon the mash on top of the sauce and use a round-bladed table knife to create a pattern on top. Drizzle over a little melted butter. Put on to a baking sheet and bake for 30-40 minutes, until bubbling and golden.

Make ahead

~ This is a great dish to make ahead. Prepare it up to a day in advance (make sure your fish is spanking fresh when you're buying, though). Cover and chill. Remove from the fridge half an hour before cooking.

Hake with salsa verde and crushed potatoes

When I took part in Celebrity Masterchef 2011, this was one of the platefuls I came up with. It is very straightforward to do and looks and tastes so fresh and lovely. There are so many reports about low fish stocks and over-fishing that it's difficult to know which fish to buy. When you're at the fish counter, look for the Marine Stewardship Council fish logo, which will be on the labels of fish that's fine to buy.

Prep: 20 minutes
Cook: 15 minutes
Serves 4

500g/1lb 2oz baby new potatoes
Salt and freshly ground black pepper
2 tbsp olive oil, plus extra to fry the fish
4 x 150g/5½oz hake fillets
2 spring onions (scallions), finely sliced
1 lemon, cut into wedges, to serve

For the salsa verde
A few sprigs each of fresh parsley, basil
   and mint
1 garlic clove
6 tbsp olive oil
1 tbsp capers
1 tsp white wine vinegar

Put the potatoes in a pan of boiling salted water. Cover and cook for around 15 minutes, until tender.

While they're cooking, make the salsa verde. Put the parsley and basil in a mini blender. Pick off the leaves from the mint and add (discarding the stems), with the garlic, olive oil, capers and vinegar. Whiz to make a thick sauce, then season to taste.

Drizzle a little oil into a frying pan and set over a medium heat. Season the fish, then fry for about 3 minutes on each side until the fish is opaque and cooked all the way through.

Drain the potatoes, then return to the pan. Add the spring onions (scallions) and 2 tbsp olive oil. Season and slice roughly with a knife. There should still be quite a few chunks in there.

Spoon the potatoes on to four plates, then add the fish. Spoon over some salsa verde and serve with a wedge of lemon.

Surprise parcels of fish

I like this way of cooking – it's a bit of a novelty and feels like a restaurant-type experience, but actually it is no bother. It's light and healthy and wrapping everything up keeps the fish and vegetables lovely and moist.

Prep: 15 minutes
Cook: 20 minutes
Serves 4

12 cherry tomatoes
½ red onion, roughly sliced
½ yellow (bell) pepper, sliced
1 courgette (zucchini), sliced
100g/3½oz asparagus tips
4 x 150g/5½oz sea bass fillets
3 tbsp white wine
3 tbsp olive oil
1 garlic clove, finely sliced
Finely grated zest of ¼ unwaxed lemon
Salt and freshly ground black pepper
Crusty bread, to serve

Preheat the oven to 200°C/180°C fan/400°F/gas mark 6.

Cut out four pieces of foil, measuring around 35 x 48cm/14 x 19in, and line each with a piece of baking parchment (around 28 x 35cm/11 x 14in). Divide the vegetables between them and top with the fish. Wrap up each parcel, leaving a little opening at the top, and then place them on two baking sheets.

Mix together the wine, olive oil, garlic and lemon zest and season well. Spoon equally between each parcel. Wrap them up to secure and cook in the oven for 20 minutes.

Slide each one on to a plate, let everyone open up their surprise, and serve with crusty bread to mop up the juices.

Fantastic roast chicken

Prep: 20 minutes
Cook: around 1¼ hours
Serves 4, with leftovers (see tip, right)

1 tomato
1 celery stick
1 carrot
½ onion
1 glass white wine
Salt and freshly ground black pepper
25g/1oz/¼ stick butter, softened
3 slices prosciutto
1 x 1.2-1.5kg/2¾lb-3lb 5oz chicken
½ lemon
2 garlic cloves
A few herb sprigs (rosemary,
   thyme, bay)
½ tbsp plain (all-purpose) flour

Love your leftovers

~ Don't chuck the carcass! There's loads of flavour left even though it has been roasted. Here's a soup my son Rory makes the day after. Pull off all the bits of meat still clinging to the bones and put them in a bowl. Put the carcass into a pan with 1ltr/1¾pt/4 cups cold water. Bring to the boil, then simmer for 20 minutes. Strain, reserving the stock. Add 2 bundles of egg noodles to the pan, the leftover chicken, 1 bashed lemongrass, a couple of slivers of fresh root ginger, 1 carrot, cut into fine matchsticks, and 2 chopped spring onions (scallions). Simmer until the noodles are cooked, and serve with a drizzle of soy sauce and chilli sauce and a few freshly chopped coriander (cilantro) leaves, if you have them.

1. Preheat the oven to 200°C/180°C fan/400°F/ gas mark 6. Roughly chop the tomato, celery, carrot and onion.

2. Put the chopped vegetables in a roasting tin. Add the wine and the equivalent volume of water and season well.

3. Chop the prosciutto, then mix together the butter and prosciutto in a bowl.

1

2

3

4. Put the chicken on a board and, using one hand to steady it, push the other up the neck end between the skin and the flesh of the breast to loosen the skin. You may need to push hard. Press the butter up into this space, squashing it to cover the breast evenly.

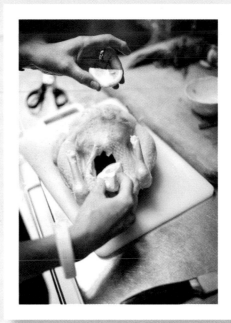

5. Place the lemon, garlic and herbs in the cavity of the chicken. Put the bird in the roasting tin. Roast for 20 minutes per 450g/1lb, plus 20 minutes. Check halfway through that there's still liquid in the tin. If it looks like it will run dry, pour boiling water in there. To check the chicken is ready, skewer the thick part of the thigh and press the flesh – the juices should be clear. If they're pink, return to the oven and check every 5 minutes.

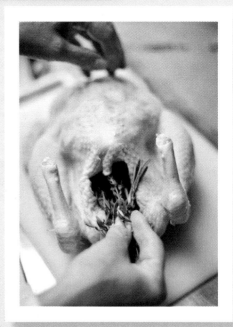

6. Take the chicken out of the tin and put on a warm platter. Cover and leave to rest. Strain the stock from the tin into a bowl, leaving the vegetables and 1 tbsp liquid. Add the flour and cook for 1-2 minutes, stirring. Return the stock to the pan, add a glass of water and cook, stirring all the time, for 2-3 minutes until syrupy. Strain the gravy into a jug. Carve the chicken, giving everyone a piece of the prosciutto-infused skin, and serve with the gravy.

Yummy creamy chicken and mushroom pie

This has become a family favourite and is good to make when you have some leftover chicken from a roast, as you just need to supplement it with a couple of extra thighs.

Prep: 30 minutes
Cook: 1 hour
Serves 4

For the pastry
200g/7oz/scant 1½ cups plain (all-purpose)
   flour, sifted, plus extra to dust
Salt and freshly ground black pepper
50g/1¾oz/scant ½ stick butter, chopped
50g/1¾oz/3½ tbsp goose fat
1 medium egg yolk, beaten, or a little milk

For the filling
3-4 chicken thighs, skinless and boneless,
   plus any leftover chopped roast chicken
600ml/1pt/2½ cups hot chicken stock
1 bay leaf
30g/1¼oz/generous ¼ stick butter
1 leek, 1 carrot and 1 celery stick, sliced
300g/10½oz potatoes, cut into bite-size pieces
A handful of button mushrooms, sliced
1 tbsp plain (all-purpose) flour
150ml/5fl oz/⅔ cup double (heavy) cream
1 tsp Dijon mustard
1 tbsp chopped fresh chives or tarragon

Make the pastry. Put the flour and a pinch of salt in a food processor. Add the fats and whiz until it looks like breadcrumbs. Add 1-2 tbsp cold water and pulse until it just comes together. Tip into a bowl and knead gently. Wrap in clingfilm and chill for 30 minutes.

Put the chicken thighs in a pan with the stock and bay. Season, cover and bring to the boil. Reduce the heat and simmer for 12-15 minutes. Melt half the butter in a separate pan and sauté the leek, carrot, celery and potatoes until golden. Season.

Whip the bay from the chicken, then chop and spoon it (plus any leftover roast chicken) and the veg into a 1.6ltr/2¾pt/3½pt ovenproof dish with the mushrooms, leaving the stock in the pan.

Preheat the oven to 200°C/180°C fan/400°F/ gas mark 6. Bring the stock to the boil and reduce to half. In a separate pan, melt the remaining butter and stir in the flour, cooking for 1 minute. Add the reduced stock, stirring. Simmer for 1-2 minutes, then add the cream, cooking for 2 minutes, until syrupy. Stir in the mustard and chives and season. Pour this over the chicken and veg.

Roll out the pastry to fit the dish on a lightly floured work surface. Put on top of the chicken and veg. Press a fork around the edge and cut two holes in the top. Brush with beaten egg or milk. Bake in the oven for 40 minutes, until golden and bubbling.

Harissa chicken and vegetable tagine

You may feel this is a labour of love when you're halfway through preparing it, but I guarantee you'll fall for its aromatic charm. The combination of spices in the tagine and chicken give a wonderful depth of flavour and really do complement each other.

Prep: 1 hour
Cook: 1½ hours
Serves 4, with leftovers

For the vegetable tagine
½ aubergine (eggplant), chopped
½ butternut squash (around 400g/14oz), peeled and roughly chopped
1 medium courgette (zucchini), roughly chopped
1 red (bell) pepper, halved, de-seeded and roughly chopped
1 red onion, roughly chopped
4 tbsp olive oil, plus extra to drizzle
Salt and freshly ground black pepper
1 large onion, grated
2 fat garlic cloves, crushed
¾ tsp cayenne pepper
1½ tbsp paprika
1½ tbsp ground ginger
1 tbsp turmeric
2 tbsp ground cinnamon
400g/14oz canned chopped tomatoes
100g/3½oz dried apricots, halved
50g/1¾oz dates, halved and pitted
50g/1¾oz sultanas (golden raisins) or raisins
50g/1¾oz flaked almonds
1 tsp saffron strands, soaked in a little cold water
600ml/1pt/2½ cups hot vegetable stock
1 tbsp clear honey
400g/14oz canned chickpeas (garbanzo beans), drained

2 tbsp roughly chopped fresh coriander (cilantro) leaves
2 tbsp roughly chopped fresh flat-leaf parsley
1 lemon, cut into wedges, to serve

For the harissa chicken
1 star anise
6 juniper berries
5 whole cloves
½ cinnamon stick
1 tbsp harissa paste
1 x 1.5kg/3lb 5oz chicken
½ lime

See next page for method...

Also try this...

~ To serve with couscous alongside, put 200g/7oz/1 cup couscous in a bowl. Add 200ml/7fl oz/scant 1 cup hot stock. Cover and leave to soak for 10 minutes. Fork through, season and add a squeeze of lemon juice and drizzle of olive oil.

~ Veggies to feed? Boil a couple of eggs until hard, then quarter and serve on top of the vegetable tagine.

To freeze

~ Any leftover tagine can be frozen. Just cool, pack in freezerproof containers and freeze for up to two months. You may need to add a splash of water when reheating it to loosen the sauce.

Harissa chicken and vegetable tagine
continued

Preheat the oven to 220°C/200°C fan/425°F/gas mark 7.

Tip the aubergine (eggplant), squash, courgette (zucchini), (bell) pepper and red onion into two separate roasting tins. Drizzle 1 tbsp olive oil over each and toss to coat. Season well. Roast for 30 minutes, then remove from the oven.

Reduce the oven temperature to 190°C/170°C fan/375°F/gas mark 5.

Meanwhile, make the harissa rub for the chicken. Put the star anise, juniper berries, cloves and cinnamon stick in a coffee mill or small blender and whiz to a fine powder. Tip into a small bowl and mix with the harissa paste.

Spatchcock (butterfly) the chicken: put it on a board and turn it breast-side down. Use a sharp knife to cut along one side of the backbone – you may need a pair of heavy-duty scissors to help with this bit. Do the same on the other side of the backbone, then discard the bone. Turn the chicken over and press the heel of your hand along the breastbone to flatten.

Put the chicken in a roasting tin. Season well, then rub it with the harissa mix, drizzle over a little oil and squeeze over the lime. Pour 100ml/3½fl oz/scant ½ cup water into the base of the tin. Place the chicken in the oven and cook for 1 hour.

Meanwhile, heat 2 tbsp oil in a large ovenproof casserole dish. Add the grated onion, garlic and spices, including 2 tsp freshly ground black pepper. Place over a medium heat and cook, stirring often, for 10 minutes, until the onion is softened but not coloured.

Add the chopped tomatoes, dried fruit, almonds, soaked saffron, stock, honey, chickpeas (garbanzo beans) and roasted veg. Give everything a really good stir and season well. Bring up to the boil. Cook in the oven underneath the chicken for 45 minutes. Check the chicken is cooked by piercing the thickest part of the thigh, and making sure the juices run clear.

Stir in the herbs and serve with the chicken, couscous (see previous page), lemon wedges and any juices from the chicken drizzled over the top.

Lamb and lentil curry with Ewan's naan

The boys are big curry lovers so here's one I knocked up for them – with a healthy twist. The lentils are wholesome and also give it a lovely earthy flavour. If you can't get hold of chana dhal (a small split yellow lentil), use the same quantity of red lentils.

Prep: 40 minutes, plus rising and proving time
Cook: 1¾–2¼ hours
Serves 4

For the lamb and lentil curry
600g/1lb 5oz lamb (leg or shoulder), cubed
1 garlic clove, crushed
A small piece of fresh root ginger, peeled and grated
1 tbsp vegetable oil
1 onion, finely chopped
1 tsp chilli powder
2 tsp ground coriander (cilantro powder)
1 tsp cumin seeds
1 tsp turmeric
2 medium tomatoes, roughly chopped
100g/3½oz/1 cup chana dhal, soaked in cold water for 30 minutes
Salt and freshly ground black pepper
800ml/27fl oz/scant 3½ cups hot vegetable stock
1 tsp tamarind paste
Fresh coriander (cilantro) leaves, roughly chopped, to serve

For the naan
300g/10½oz/generous 2 cups plain (all-purpose) flour, plus extra for rolling out
½ tsp fast-action dried (active dry) yeast
1 tsp salt
75g/2¾oz/1 cup plain yogurt
1 tbsp butter

See next page for method...

Also try this...

~ I serve curry with a bowl of yogurt, plus a red onion, cucumber and tomato salsa.

~ Serve with basmati rice – 250g/9oz/1⅓ cups is enough for four people.

Lamb and lentil curry
with Ewan's naan continued

Put the lamb in a sealable container and add the garlic and ginger. Cover and chill overnight if you have time. Otherwise just set aside while you start cooking.

Heat the oil over a medium heat and fry the onion for about 8-10 minutes until golden – it's important it gets a bit of colour, as this adds depth of flavour to the finished curry. Add the lamb and cook until brown on all sides.

Add the spices and cook for a good 5 minutes, adding a drizzle of boiling water if the pan looks dry. Add the tomatoes and dhal and stir.

Season well. Pour over the stock, cover and bring to the boil. Reduce the heat to a simmer, then cook for 1½-2 hours, or until the lamb is tender and the sauce has reduced. Stir in the tamarind paste.

While the lamb is cooking, make the naan. Sift the flour into a large bowl and add the yeast and salt. Mix the yogurt with 175ml/6fl oz/¾ cup water, then make a well in the centre of flour and stir everything together with a knife. Tip on to a clean, floured work surface and knead until soft and sticky.

Return to the bowl, cover and allow to rise for 1 hour.

Preheat the grill (broiler) and put a baking sheet under to preheat.

Divide the dough into four pieces on a clean, lightly floured work surface. Roll one piece into a round, then hold one end and, with the rolling pin, roll the other end until it naturally widens at the bottom. The piece should measure 22cm/8½in long and 13cm/5in wide at the thickest part, in a traditional teardrop shape. Do the same with the other pieces of dough. Allow to prove for 10 minutes.

Melt the butter in a pan over a medium heat. When the butter is foaming, skim off the white bits that float to the top, leaving the clear butter underneath.

Dust the hot baking sheet with flour, then grill (broil) the naan in two batches for 2-3 minutes on each side until they're dotted with brown spots. Place on a wire rack and brush with the clarified butter.

Sprinkle the curry with fresh coriander (cilantro) and serve with the naan.

Baked lamb chops

This all-in-one-pan dish is one of my mum's regulars and I love it for its rich, dark deliciousness, together with the sweetness of the vegetables. It's an old-fashioned way of cooking, because there's no hint of pinkness – the meat is done until it's falling off the bone – but that for me is its appeal.

Prep: 15 minutes
Cook: 2 hours
Serves 4

8 lamb chops
1 sweet potato (around 450g/1lb),
   roughly chopped
1 large carrot, sliced
1 red (bell) pepper, cut into chunks
1 onion, cut into chunks
1 tsp Marmite (yeast extract)
800ml/27fl oz/scant 3½ cups hot
   chicken stock
Salt and freshly ground black pepper
Mashed potato, to serve (see page 160)

Preheat the oven to 190°C/170°C fan/375°F/ gas mark 5.

Put the lamb chops in a large roasting tin. Add the sweet potato, carrot, pepper and onion, making sure each is evenly distributed around the tin. The meat and vegetables should, more or less, sit in an even layer. Stir the Marmite (yeast extract) into the stock, then pour over the chops. Season well.

Cover the tin with foil and cook in the oven for 1 hour. Remove the foil, then continue to cook for another hour, until the lamb is gorgeously brown on top and tender – it should pull away from the bone easily with a fork.

Divide between four plates and serve with mashed potato.

Also try this...

~ Use the second shelf of the oven to roast some veg for another meal. Chop everything into chunks – aubergine (eggplant), pepper, onion, carrot or other root vegetable and squash are all good – and put in a large roasting tin. Drizzle with oil. Toss well and season, then cook underneath the lamb until tender (it should take around 1 hour).

Sunday-best pork fillet with special boulangère potatoes

Here's a recipe we made up one Sunday with leftover bits in the bottom of the fridge and spices from the drawer. It's a great way of tarting up a pork fillet – and cooking it on top of a bed of vegetables, wine and water leaves the meat lovely and moist. The resulting juices in the tin don't make a lot of gravy, but it's full of flavour.

Prep: 30 minutes
Cook: 1½ hours
Serves 4, with leftovers (see tip below)

For the boulangère potatoes
1kg/2¼lb waxy maincrop potatoes, sliced
1 onion, finely sliced
½ fennel bulb, finely sliced
1 garlic clove, sliced
Salt and freshly ground black pepper
40g/1½oz/3 tbsp butter
600ml/1pt/2½ cups hot chicken stock

For the pork
600g/1lb 5oz pork tenderloin
1 tbsp fennel seeds
2 garlic cloves
2 tbsp olive oil
1 celery stick, roughly chopped
1 carrot, roughly chopped
1 tomato, roughly chopped
½ onion, roughly chopped
A glass of white wine
A knob (pat) of butter
½ tbsp plain (all-purpose) flour

Preheat the oven to 200°C/180°C fan/400°F/ gas mark 6.

Layer up the potatoes in a 2ltr/3½pt/good 2 quart ovenproof dish, slotting in the onion, fennel and garlic as you go. Season between each layer. Stir the butter into the stock and pour all over. Cover loosely with foil and cook in the oven for 1½ hours, or until the potatoes are tender. (Halfway through, take off the foil and press the potatoes with a large metal spoon so the top ones soak up some of the buttery stock again, then re-cover and continue to cook.)

Meanwhile, for the pork, whiz the fennel seeds, garlic, 1 tsp salt and the olive oil in a mini blender or spice mill. Slice the pork fillet along its length, taking care not to cut all the way through. Spoon the spice mixture into the split and tie up with string (don't tie it too tightly, otherwise the filling will spill out).

Put the chopped vegetables in the bottom of a roasting tin and sit the pork on top. Pour in enough water to cover the bottom of the pan by 2cm/¾in. Add the wine.

Continued overleaf...

Sunday-best pork fillet with special boulangère potatoes continued

Put into the oven above the potatoes and roast for around 1 hour. Take the pork out of the oven and turn the oven up to its highest setting. Put the pork on a warm plate and cover to keep warm.

Remove the foil from the potatoes, then move them up a rack in the oven and continue to cook for 10 minutes to brown on top.

Strain the stock from the pork roasting tin and add the butter and flour to the tin. Cook over a medium-high heat for 1-2 minutes. Slowly pour in the reserved stock, stirring all the time. Simmer until syrupy – this won't take long – then strain.

Slice the pork and serve with a spoonful of the potatoes and a little of the gravy over the top.

American-style baked ham and beans

Here's a top-notch supper that wins all round. It's easy on the washing-up (it's cooked in a roasting tin) and the oven does all the work – well, bar a bit of browning of the meat at the beginning. Plus the leftovers can be made into another meal. What's not to love?

Prep: 15 minutes
Cook: 1¾ hours
Serves 4

1 tbsp olive oil
1.2kg/2¾lb gammon joint
1 onion, roughly chopped
800g/1¾lb canned cannellini or haricot
　beans, drained
400g/14oz canned chopped tomatoes
300ml/10fl oz/1¼ cups hot vegetable or
　chicken stock
1 tbsp tomato ketchup
1 tsp Dijon mustard
2 splashes Worcestershire sauce
25g/1oz/scant ¼ cup soft light brown sugar
1 tbsp red wine vinegar
Salt and freshly ground black pepper

Love your leftovers

~ Place the cooled portion of ham in an airtight container, cool, then cover and chill for up to three days. Enjoy with hasselback potatoes and coleslaw (see opposite).

Preheat the oven to 180°C/160°C fan/350°F/ gas mark 4.

Heat the oil in a flameproof roasting tin over a medium heat and brown the gammon all over, cooking the joint fat-side down first. Don't worry if the meat feels as if it's sticking to the pan initially; just wait for the heat to brown it, then it will release itself easily.

Add the onion, beans, tomatoes, stock, ketchup, mustard, Worcestershire sauce, sugar and vinegar to the pan. Season and stir everything together. Bring the mixture up to a bubble on the heat. Turn off the heat, cover the whole tin with foil and bake in the oven for 1½ hours.

Ten minutes before the end of cooking, remove the foil, then finish off in the oven.

Lift the joint out of the tin and put it on a board. Cut it in half and cool one piece (see tip, left). Slice the remaining half, divide between four shallow bowls and serve each with a good spoonful of the beans.

Cold ham with hasselback potatoes and coleslaw

Make the American-style baked ham and beans (opposite) and you'll be halfway to having this on the table. It's also a great dish to do around Christmas time, when you've had enough of rich food but you still have bits and bobs in the fridge that need using up.

Prep: 20 minutes
Cook: 1 hour
Serves 4

Around 500g/1lb 2oz leftover cold ham
  (see opposite)

For the hasselback potatoes
900g/2lb new potatoes
3 tbsp olive oil
25g/1oz/¼ stick butter
Salt and freshly ground black pepper

For the coleslaw
¼ red cabbage, finely chopped
½ red onion, finely chopped
2 spring onions (scallions), finely chopped
1 apple, cored and finely chopped
15g/½oz pumpkin seeds, toasted
1 tbsp mayonnaise
2 tbsp plain yogurt
1 tbsp olive oil
2 tsp red wine vinegar
2 tbsp chopped fresh parsley

Preheat the oven to 200°C/180°C fan/400°F/ gas mark 6.

Use a sharp knife to cut slits along the width of the potatoes, slicing around two-thirds of the way through. Put in the roasting tin and toss in the oil. Put a little bit of butter on top of each potato, and season with salt and pepper. Roast for 1 hour, tossing the pan halfway through.

Meanwhile, put the cabbage, red onion, spring onions (scallions), apple and pumpkin seeds into a large bowl. Mix together the mayonnaise, yogurt, oil, vinegar and parsley in a separate bowl and season. Pour over the vegetable mixture and toss together well.

Slice the ham.

When the potatoes are ready, the cuts will have fanned out nicely and they'll be deliciously golden. Divide between four plates and serve with the leftover ham slices and the coleslaw.

Quick-braised oxtail

My mum used to cook this a lot when we were growing up, and I adore its richness and deliciousness. Cooking oxtail from scratch to get to the stage of melting and unctuous soft meat that slides off the bone takes a good half-day. Using a pressure cooker slashes the time drastically, without compromising on flavour.

Prep: 40 minutes
Cook: 1 hour 20 minutes
Serves 4

For the stew
1 tbsp vegetable oil
1 onion, finely chopped
1 carrot, finely chopped
1 celery stick, finely chopped
Salt and freshly ground black pepper
1.2kg/2¾lb oxtail (4 big and 4 tiny
    end pieces)
1 tbsp plain (all-purpose) flour
100ml/3½fl oz/scant ½ cup port
600ml/1pt/2½ cups hot beef stock
1 bay leaf

For the mash
1kg/2¼lb potatoes
A knob (pat) of butter
A splash of milk

Heat the oil in a large frying pan (skillet) and quickly cook the onion, carrot and celery for 8-10 minutes over a medium heat until they are starting to turn golden at the edges. Tip into the pressure cooker.

Season the oxtail, then brown it in batches in the same pan until it is golden all over.

Method continued overleaf

Also try this...

~ If you prefer a thicker gravy, remove all the meat from the pan and bring the sauce up to the boil. Bubble for around 5 minutes, until thickened and syrupy.

To freeze

~ This freezes well. Just pick all the meat off the bone, discarding any gelatinous bits, and add to the sauce. Put in a plastic sealable container and freeze for up to three months. Thaw overnight and heat thoroughly to serve.

Quick-braised oxtail

Add the oxtail to the vegetables. Sprinkle over the flour and stir it in.

Add the port to the pressure cooker and, using a wooden spoon, stir it all together.

Pour in the stock, and then tuck the bay down the side of the pan.

Give everything a good stir, then bring to the boil. Secure the lid on the pressure cooker and bring it up to full pressure over a high heat. Once the cooker is at pressure, reduce the heat to medium-low and cook for 1 hour.

Halfway through the cooking time, make the mash. Put the potatoes into a large pan of cold, salted water. Cover, bring to the boil then reduce the heat to a simmer and cook for 20-25 minutes until tender. Drain well. Return the potatoes to the pan and heat to drive off any steam, then mash with the butter and milk. Check the seasoning.

Turn off the hob and release the pressure. Divide the mash between four plates, then top each with two pieces of oxtail and some gravy.

Matthew's meatballs
with homemade pasta

This is one of my all-time favourite things to eat. I consider it my ex-husband Matthew's signature dish, and it would be my chosen last supper. Making pasta from scratch may seem like a faff but it's worth it. Don't invest in a machine; you can use a rolling pin.

Prep: 1 hour 20 minutes
Cook: 50 minutes
Serves 4

For the pasta
300g/10½oz/2 cups '00' pasta flour, sifted
3 medium eggs

For the sauce
2 tbsp olive oil
1 small onion, finely chopped
1 bacon rasher (strip), roughly chopped
2 garlic cloves, crushed
1 sprig of fresh rosemary, finely chopped
400g/14oz canned chopped tomatoes
1 bay leaf
A splash of red wine
200ml/7fl oz/scant 1 cup hot chicken stock

For the meatballs
1 small onion, roughly chopped
A good handful of fresh parsley
450g/1lb minced (ground) beef
1 small egg, beaten
2 tbsp matzo meal, plus some for coating
1 tbsp olive oil, for frying
salt and freshly ground black pepper

Put the flour in a food processor and crack in the eggs. Whiz. Tip on to a surface and knead for 1-2 minutes. Wrap in clingfilm and rest in a cool place for 30 minutes. Unwrap the dough and cut it into quarters. Roll each piece out to 1-2mm/¹⁄₁₆in thick. Cut into 5mm/¼in strips. Dust a big plate with flour and put the strips on it.

Make the sauce. Heat the oil in a large, wide pan over a medium heat. Add the onion and bacon and cook for 10 minutes. Stir in the garlic and cook for 1 minute. Add the rosemary, tomatoes and bay. Season, cover and simmer on low for 20 minutes.

Make the meatballs. Put the onion and parsley in a mini blender and whiz. Tip into a bowl and add the mince, egg and matzo meal. Season. Mix with your hands. Sprinkle the extra matzo meal on to a plate. Take walnut-sized pieces and shape into balls. Roll in the matzo meal. Fry in the oil in batches until golden, then set aside.

Deglaze the pan with wine. Add the sauce and meatballs. Add enough stock to almost cover the meatballs. Stir. Cover. Cook for 30 minutes, turning the meatballs halfway through. Boil the pasta in salted water for 3-4 minutes. Drain, leaving a little water clinging to it. Divide between four plates. Spoon the sauce and meatballs over.

Fresh air food

Fresh air food

Vegetable empanadas

I had the opportunity to visit Buenos Aires when I took part in the TV series 'Total Wipeout'. While it was (sort of) fun doing that, I also had a great time trying some of Argentina's national dishes – this is one I particularly enjoyed.

Prep: 30 minutes, plus 1 hour chilling
Cook: 50 minutes
Makes 6

For the pastry
300g/10½oz/generous 2 cups plain
   (all-purpose) flour, plus extra for
   rolling out
½ tsp salt
100g/3½oz/7 tbsp white vegetable fat
   (vegetable shortening), chopped
1 medium egg, beaten

For the filling
1 tbsp vegetable or olive oil
4 spring onions (scallions), chopped
½ red (bell) pepper, cut into small pieces
300g/10½oz potatoes, cut into small pieces
2 garlic cloves, finely sliced
A pinch of chilli flakes or a knifepoint
   of smoked paprika
Salt and freshly ground black pepper
200ml/7fl oz/scant 1 cup vegetable stock
1 tbsp tomato purée (paste)
2 generous handfuls of spinach leaves

For the pastry, sift the flour into a large bowl and add the salt. Add the vegetable fat (shortening) and rub in (or use a food processor) until the mixture resembles breadcrumbs. Stir in enough cold water to make a soft dough. Bring together and knead. Shape into a disc, wrap in clingfilm (plastic wrap) and chill for 1 hour.

Make the filling. Heat the oil in a small pan and add the spring onions (scallions), pepper and potatoes. Cook for 5-10 minutes. Add the garlic, chilli and seasoning and stir. Cook for 1-2 minutes.

Add the stock and tomato purée (paste) and cover. Bring to the boil, then turn the heat down low and cook for 10-15 minutes until the potatoes are tender. If it looks a bit dry, drizzle over a little water. Add the spinach, cover and allow to wilt down.

Preheat the oven to 200°C/180°C fan/400°F/gas mark 6. Divide the dough into six pieces on a lightly floured surface. Roll out one piece to a circle 16cm/6¼in diameter. Spoon a sixth of the filling into the middle of a circle, brush the edge with beaten egg and fold over. Press with a fork around the edge, then cut two slits in the top. Place on a baking sheet. Repeat to make six empanadas. Brush with the remaining egg. Bake for 30 minutes. Cool for 10 minutes.

Also try this...

~ If you're making these for omnivores, you can throw in a bit of shredded cooked chicken or pork with the spinach cooked for the filling.

Love your leftovers

~ They'll keep in an airtight container in a cool place for up to two days, but not in the fridge as the pastry will harden.

Real tabbouleh

I live off this in the summer. It's so quick to make, lasts a few days in the fridge and is packed full of those healthy fresh-tasting ingredients we all love. It's also a great sidekick to chicken, fish, griddled halloumi, lamb...the list could go on.

**Prep: 15 minutes, plus at least
30 minutes' soaking time
Serves 4**

150g/5½oz/1 cup cracked wheat
    (bulgur wheat)
Juice of 1 lemon
4 spring onions (scallions), finely chopped
½ cucumber, peeled, halved, de-seeded
    and finely chopped
2 tomatoes, halved, de-seeded and
    finely chopped
2-3 tbsp extra virgin olive oil
A big spoonful of black olives,
    pitted and chopped
A handful of fresh mint, roughly chopped
A handful of fresh flat-leaf parsley,
    roughly chopped
Salt and freshly ground black pepper
Lemon wedges, to serve

Put the cracked wheat into a large shallow bowl. Pour the lemon juice into a jug and make up to 300ml/10fl oz/ 1¼ cups with boiling water. Pour over the wheat, cover and leave to soak and cool for at least 30 minutes.

When the wheat has cooled, stir in the remaining ingredients and season well. Toss everything together and serve immediately with lemon wedges.

Make ahead

~ If you want to prepare this in advance, it will keep well in the fridge for up to two days.

Loaded focaccia

I adore bread and I love Italian food, and this loaf is the best combination of the two. I've been making it for years and never tire of it.

**Prep: 30 minutes, plus 1 hour
  rising and proving time
Cook: 40 minutes
Makes 1 handsome loaf**

600g/1lb 5oz/4¼ cups strong white
  bread flour, plus extra for rolling out
12g/a good ¼oz fast-action dried
  (active dry) yeast
1½ tsp salt
5 tbsp olive oil, plus extra for drizzling
1 small red onion, finely sliced
Leaves from a fresh rosemary sprig
225g/8oz new potatoes
2 tbsp freshly grated Parmesan

Sift the flour into a large bowl. Stir in the yeast and salt. Make a well in the centre, add the olive oil and pour in 400ml/14fl oz/1¾ cups lukewarm water. Mix with a knife to make a rough dough, then tip on to a board and knead until smooth and sticky. Put back in the bowl, cover and set aside for 40 minutes. (You can also do this in a freestanding mixer using a dough hook.)

Line a 20 x 30cm/8 x 12in roasting tin with baking parchment. When the dough has risen, scrape it out into the prepared tin. Roughly stretch it and knead it until it fills the tin. Set aside to prove for 20 minutes.

Preheat the oven to 200°C/180°C fan/400°F/ gas mark 6.

Push your fingers all over the dough to create little holes. Toss the onion and rosemary in a little oil to coat, then scatter evenly over the top of the dough. Finely slice the potatoes (a mandolin is best for this) over the top to cover, each slice slightly overlapping the other. Season well and drizzle over a little oil. Sprinkle over the Parmesan.

Bake for 40 minutes until it is golden all around the edges and sounds hollow when lightly tapped on top. You may need to turn the tin round halfway through, depending on how your oven browns.

Remove from the oven and lift the bread out, using the parchment as support. Place it on a wire rack, removing the parchment, and then leave to cool. Drizzle with a little extra oil.

Fantastic potato salad

Our picnics wouldn't be the same without this. It's a happy combination of all those ingredients that I have sitting in the fridge in the summer. It's fine to make this up to a day ahead, too, and easy to multiply up if you need to feed more.

Prep: 10 minutes
Cook: 10 minutes
Serves 4

600g/1lb 5oz new potatoes,
   chopped into small pieces
2 tbsp mayonnaise
2 tbsp plain yogurt
3 tbsp olive oil
2 spring onions (scallions), finely chopped
1 tbsp baby capers
4 cocktail gherkins, roughly chopped
A small handful of fresh parsley,
   roughly chopped
A sprig of fresh mint, roughly chopped
½ fresh red chilli pepper, finely chopped
Salt and freshly ground black pepper

Put the potatoes in a pan of boiling water. Cover and bring to the boil, then cook for 8-10 minutes until tender. Drain well, then cool until just warm.

Put the remaining ingredients into a large bowl and season well. Add the potatoes and toss to coat, tasting a chunk of potato to check the seasoning.

Take-anywhere Spanish omelette

Just a handful of ingredients goes into this simple yet yummy crowd-pleaser. It's ideal picnic fare: it transports easily and tastes just as good cold as it does freshly made.

Prep: 15 minutes
Cook: around 30 minutes
Serves 4

5½ tbsp olive oil
1 large onion, finely chopped
600g/1lb 5oz potatoes, cut into 1cm/1½in dice
4 large eggs
Salt and freshly ground black pepper

Heat 5 tbsp of the oil in a small frying pan (skillet), measuring 18cm/7in across on the base. Add the onion and potatoes (peeled if you prefer) and fry over a medium heat for 15 minutes, turning and tossing the ingredients from time to time until tender. Spoon into a sieve resting over a bowl to drain off the oil.

Beat the eggs in a separate bowl and season well. Add the potato mixture and toss together. Preheat the grill (broiler).

Heat the remaining ½ tbsp oil in the same frying pan and, when hot, add the eggy mixture, spreading it out in an even layer. Cook gently until golden underneath and almost set on top – around 5 minutes. Use a palette knife to slip down the edge of the omelette to check the colour underneath.

Finish off under the grill (broiler) and take care to cook until only just set. It should still be a little moist – you don't want it dry and rubbery. Upturn on to a plate and serve.

Love your leftovers
~ If you don't eat it all, it will keep in the fridge in an airtight container for up to two days.

Puff pastry pissaladière

This mouthful of gorgeousness is so easy to make and is based on the French Provençal recipe, with my ex-husband Matthew's twist using puff pastry. It's important to preheat the baking sheet first, then slide the prepared tart on to it and put it straight into the oven to ensure the base is lovely and crisp.

Prep: 20 minutes
Cook: 1 hour
Serves 4-8

2 tbsp olive oil
40g/1½oz/3 tbsp butter
4 onions, finely sliced
Salt and freshly ground black pepper
½ x 500g/1lb 2oz block puff pastry or a
   250g/9oz ready-rolled puff pastry sheet
Plain (all-purpose) flour, for dusting
Around 12 anchovies, drained of oil
8-9 black olives, halved and pitted
A few sprigs of fresh thyme

Make ahead
~ You can prepare the onions up to two days ahead. Spoon into an airtight container, then cool and chill.

To freeze
~ Wrap the other half of the puff pastry in clingfilm (plastic wrap) and freeze for up to a month.

Put the oil and butter in a large pan and add the onions. Season well and place over a medium heat. When the butter has melted, give the onions a good stir. Cover with a piece of greaseproof (wax) paper that's been scrunched up, wetted, then pulled apart again, and put a lid on top. Cook over a low heat for 40 minutes, stirring every now and then, and adding a drizzle of water if it needs it. Tip into a sieve resting over a bowl to cool and strain away any liquid.

Preheat the oven to 220°C/200°C fan/425°F/ gas mark 7. Place a heavy baking sheet inside it to heat up.

Lightly dust a piece of baking parchment with flour, then roll out the pastry on top using short quick strokes until it measures around 24 x 30cm/9½ x 12in. Trim the edges. Spoon the onion evenly over the top, then dress with the anchovies in a criss-cross pattern. Put half an olive in the middle of each diamond. Season well and sprinkle with the thyme leaves.

Slide the parchment on to the preheated baking sheet and bake the tart for 20 minutes. Cool a little, then slide on to a board, slice and serve.

Sorrelle's salmon cutlets

My late mother-in-law used to make these often, using tinned salmon – they were a favourite of her son's. Now he goes fishing in the summer and brings back lots of river trout. Any leftovers are turned into these toothsome morsels, best served with a potato salad (see page 174).

Prep: 15 minutes
Cook: 15 minutes
Serves 4

A good handful of fresh parsley
1 small onion, roughly chopped
About 250g/9oz canned or cooked
   salmon or trout, flaked
1 medium egg, beaten
Salt and freshly ground black pepper
2 tbsp medium matzo meal, plus extra
   to coat
Vegetable oil

Put the parsley and onion in a blender and whiz it to mince the ingredients together. Tip into a bowl and use a fork to mix in the fish and beaten egg. Season well.

Add the matzo meal. If you have a small amount of fish, you'll need more meal; the important thing is that it should be dry enough to be able to shape, but still slightly sticky. Add enough to achieve this and shape the mixture into ovals about 4cm/1½in long (this bit is good fun for the kids to do). Put some matzo meal on a plate and roll the ovals in this.

Heat some oil in a frying pan (skillet) or saucepan – you can either deep- or shallow-fry them – and cook the cutlets in batches for 4 minutes, turning them over if you're shallow-frying.

Serve hot straight from the pan with a little sprinkle of salt, or at room temperature.

Sage and onion sausage rolls

This is my picnic standby. I always have sage in the garden and that's what makes these taste so gorgeous. I used to enjoy making them for my dad – he loved them.

Prep: 20 minutes
Cook: 20 minutes
Makes 30

500g/1lb 2oz pork sausagemeat
1 shallot, finely chopped
1 tbsp roughly chopped fresh sage
1 medium egg, plus 1 large yolk
Salt and freshly ground black pepper
500g/1lb 2oz puff pastry
Plain (all-purpose) flour, to dust

Preheat the oven to 200°C/180°C fan/400°F/ gas mark 6.

Put the sausagemeat, shallot, sage, whole egg and seasoning in a bowl and mix well. Roll out the pastry on a lightly floured board to measure 30 x 50cm/12 x 20in.

Divide the sausagemeat into three portions and roughly mould each piece into a sausage shape, using a little plain (all-purpose) flour, to fit the width of the pastry. Space the sausagemeat lengths evenly from top to bottom on the pastry, then cut along the pastry between them.

Beat the egg yolk with 1 tbsp water, then brush egg along the bottom edge of each strip. Roll each up, tucking in the top layer of pastry so it sticks on the yolk, to make three long rolls.

Lift on to a baking sheet (you may need to trim the length of the rolls to fit it at this stage), then brush with the remaining yolk.

Now take a sharp knife and cut a little way into the rolls at 5cm/2in intervals. Prick the tops with a fork and bake for 30-35 minutes or until golden. Cool on a wire rack, cut up and serve or pack for a picnic.

Marinated lamb kebabs

These are delicious. The red onion gives the lamb bite, while the lemon softens and provides a citrus kick. Serve with a yogurt, cucumber and mint dip.

Prep: 20 minutes,
  plus 2 hours' marinating
Cook: 10-20 minutes
Serves 4

500g/1lb 2oz lamb leg meat, trimmed
  and cut into 2.5cm/1in pieces
1 tbsp sherry or red wine vinegar
1 tbsp chopped fresh oregano
½ garlic clove, crushed
1 tbsp olive oil
¼ red onion, cut into 4 wedges
1 lemon
Salt and freshly ground black pepper

Soak eight wooden skewers in cold water.

Put the lamb in a non-metallic container. Add the vinegar, oregano, garlic, oil and onion. Halve the lemon and squeeze the juice of one half over the top. Toss all the ingredients together. Cut the other lemon half into eight wedges and put into the container, too. Cover and chill. Marinate for up to 2 hours.

Preheat the grill (broiler) to medium-hot.

Thread five or six pieces of lamb on to one of the skewers. Break up a wedge of onion into two smaller pieces, then thread one of them on to the end. Push a wedge of lemon on to the end. Repeat to make up all eight skewers. Season well.

Cook under the grill (broiler) for 10 minutes, turning halfway through, until the meat is cooked. Serve with salad.

Also try this...

~ You can also do these on the barbecue. Wait until the coals are covered in white ash and it's ready to go.

Brilliant bangers

'Sticky willies' were a staple of every Good Housekeeping party when I worked there. They're incredibly moreish and get gobbled up in direct relation to how much booze is consumed. Also really quick to throw together for a picnic or summer party.

Prep: 20 minutes
Cook: 20 minutes
Serves 4

18 chipolata (small pork) sausages
1 tbsp thick-set honey
1 tbsp soy sauce
2 tsp Dijon mustard
1 tbsp sesame seeds
1 tbsp hoisin sauce

Preheat the oven to 200°C/180°C fan/400°F/ gas mark 6.

Put the sausages in a large roasting tin, add everything else and give it a stir to coat the sausages in the mixture.

Roast for 20 minutes, giving the tin a good shake and tossing the sausages in the sticky goo halfway through.

Spoon into a dish and enjoy warm.

Failsafe flapjacks

Here's a home-baked treat that anyone can make, as it doesn't call for special ingredients or equipment. I've made this recipe so they're syrupy and firm with a lovely chewy texture. You need to mark them as soon as they come out of the oven, and leave them in the tin to cool completely, otherwise they won't stick together.

Prep: 10 minutes
Cook: 20 minutes
Makes 16 rather moreish squares

125g/4½oz/1 generous stick butter,
   plus extra to grease
100g/3½oz/½ cup golden caster
   (superfine) sugar
3 tbsp golden (light corn) syrup
225g/8oz/2⅔ cups porridge (rolled) oats

Preheat the oven to 180°/160°C fan/350°F/ gas mark 4. Grease a square cake tin with a base measurement of 17cm/6½in.

Put the butter in a small pan with the sugar and syrup. Place over a low heat to melt the butter and stir to combine. Add the oats to the pan and mix well to coat the oats with the butter mixture. Spoon into the prepared tin and level the top with the back of a metal spoon.

Bake for 15 minutes until just golden. Remove from the oven, mark into squares and leave to cool completely in the tin. As the buttery mixture cools, it'll set the oats so they're easy to cut out into squares.

Cut and lift out with a palette knife and store in an airtight container for up to five days.

Also try this...

~ I love flapjacks but with all the butter and sugar, it's good to add a handful of raisins or chopped dried apricots to assuage the guilt.

Anyone for pud?

Anyone for pud?

No-fuss queen of puddings

This is one of those dishes that goes in and out of fashion, but it's always on my list of favourites – so simple and nothing special to be bought. I made this for ITV's 'Britain's Best Dish' a couple of years ago, and all the judges said it tasted wonderful.

Prep: 15 minutes
Cook: 40 minutes
Serves 4

For the base
Butter, for greasing
450ml/16fl oz/2 cups full-fat milk
Finely grated zest of 1 large
    unwaxed lemon
40g/1½ oz/2½ tbsp golden caster
    (superfine) sugar
90g/3¼oz/scant 2 cups good-quality
    white breadcrumbs
½ vanilla pod, split along the
    length
3 large egg yolks
3 tbsp good-quality seedless
    raspberry jam

For the meringue
3 large egg whites
150g/5½oz/¾ cup golden caster
    (superfine) sugar, plus a little extra
    to sprinkle over

1. Preheat the oven to 180°C/160°C fan/350°F/gas mark 4. Butter a fairly shallow 1.2ltr/2pt/2½pt ovenproof dish. Make the base: in a saucepan bring the milk to just below the boil. Stir in the lemon zest and sugar.

2. Add the breadcrumbs and vanilla.

3. Allow to cool a little, then beat in the egg yolks.

4. Remove the pod and pour the mixture into the prepared dish. Bake for around 20 minutes until set (but not rigid). Put to one side and turn up the oven to 190°C/170°C fan/375°F/gas mark 5.

1

2

3

4

5-6. Melt the jam and spread over the base.

7. For the meringue, beat the whites with an electric whisk until fairly stiff. Continue whisking and gradually add the sugar, a tablespoon at a time at first, then increase as the meringue bulks up. Pile it over the base, using the back of the spoon to make it look beautiful and swirly.

8. Sprinkle the meringue with a little sugar and stick it back in the oven for about 12-15 minutes until nicely coloured. Serve warm rather than hot.

Sumptuous marinated peaches

This sums up summer to me: fresh, fragrant peaches married together with tart raspberries and bathed in a sweet lemon and wine syrup. If you can't get hold of peaches, use nectarines instead.

**Prep time: 15 minutes, plus at least
  1 hour marinating**
Serves 4

3-4 ripe white peaches
150g/5½oz raspberries
Juice of ¼ lemon
3 tbsp golden caster (superfine) sugar
100ml/3½fl oz/scant ½ cup dry white wine

Cut a cross in the top and bottom of each peach and put it in a bowl. Pour over boiling water. Allow the fruit to sit for 1 minute, then peel, slice and put them in a serving bowl.

Add the raspberries to the bowl. Mix together the lemon juice, sugar and white wine and pour over the fruit.

Chill for at least 1 hour, stirring every now and then, then serve.

Also try this...

~ If you want to serve this to children, swap the wine with the same quantity of orange juice.

Banana ice cream

This recipe came about from a gorgeous Sunday lunch we all had in a Buckinghamshire restaurant a couple of years back. Rory and I ordered the banana ice cream, which was divine. I asked if I could have the recipe, then waited and waited until I realized it wasn't going to materialize. When I got home I rustled this up while the flavours were fresh in my mind, and was dead chuffed when it turned out pretty much as I had wanted it to.

Prep time: 20 minutes, plus cooling, churning and freezing
Serves 4

300ml/10fl oz/1¼ cups double cream (heavy cream)
3 large egg yolks
75g/2¾oz/ scant ½ cup golden caster sugar (superfine sugar)
300g/10½oz bananas (peeled weight)
2 tbsp dark rum
Freshly grated nutmeg
1 tbsp lemon juice

Pour the cream into a small pan and bring to the boil to scald it, then turn off the heat.

Mix the yolks and sugar together in a bowl and pour in the cream, stirring all the time. Rinse the pan, then return the mixture to it. Gently cook over a low heat, stirring all the time, until slightly thickened and custard-like – it should coat the back of the spoon. Remove from the heat

Mash the bananas in a bowl, add the rum and grate over some nutmeg. Stir in the lemon juice and the custard.

Chill then churn in an ice cream machine until firm. Freeze until ready to enjoy.

To freeze
~ If you don't have an ice cream machine, pour the chilled mixture into a shallow freezerproof container and freeze. Stir every hour to break up any ice crystals and keep it smooth.

Eggy bread with fudgey plums

I love puddings and this is one of my favourites, particularly as it doesn't need any hard-to-find ingredients. You can use whatever you have in the fruit bowl. Plus it's dead quick when you haven't planned a pud and you need to get something on the table fast.

Prep: 10 minutes
Cook: 15 minutes
Serves 4

3 medium eggs
2 tbsp golden caster (superfine) sugar
8 small slices bread
A little butter and drizzle of vegetable oil, plus extra if needed

For the plums
75g/2¾oz/⅔ stick butter
4 plums, halved and pitted
Juice of 1 orange
75g/2¾oz/ scant ½ cup soft light brown sugar
150-200ml/5-7fl oz/⅔-¾ cup double (heavy) cream
1 tsp vanilla extract

Beat the eggs in a shallow dish with the sugar. Add the bread slices in batches and allow each to soak up some of the eggy mixture.

For the plums, melt the butter in a large pan. Add the fruit, cut-side down, pour over the orange juice and cook gently for around 5 minutes until softened, turning over halfway. Remove the plums from the pan and keep to one side. Add the sugar, cream and vanilla to the pan and cook until caramelized and saucy.

While the sauce is cooking, heat the butter and oil in a large frying pan (skillet). Cook the soaked and drained bread in batches until golden on each side, adding more butter or oil if the pan's looking dry.

Divide the slices between four plates, top with two plum halves and drizzle a little of the sauce over each.

Also try this...

~ Plums are my favourite fruit for this, but you could also use apples, pears, mangoes or bananas.

~ I've used two types of sugar for this recipe. If you don't have any soft light brown sugar, you can use golden caster (superfine). It will just be less rich.

Ewan's deep and chunky apple pie

Who doesn't love apple pie? My son Ewan has perfected this recipe, with help from his dad, and I think it's very special. The secret is the way he cooks the apples so they're tender but still retain their shape and don't go all mushy inside the dish.

Prep: 40 minutes,
**   plus chilling**
Cook: 40 minutes
Serves 4-6

For the sweet shortcrust pastry
300g/10½oz/generous 2 cups
    plain (all-purpose) flour,
    plus extra for rolling out
150g/5½oz/1⅓ sticks butter,
    diced and chilled
2 tbsp golden caster
    (superfine) sugar
2 medium egg yolks

For the filling
1.4kg/3lb Bramley apples
    (baking apples), cored and
    sliced
75g/2¾oz/ scant ½ cup golden caster (superfine),
    sugar, plus extra to sprinkle
3-4 whole cloves
1-2 tbsp apricot jam
1 medium egg, beaten

1. Make the pastry. Put the flour, butter and sugar into a food processor and whiz until the mixture resembles breadcrumbs.

2. Beat the egg yolks together with 4 tbsp cold water. Drizzle over the flour mixture and pulse until it looks as if it's about to come together.

3. Tip out on to a clean, lightly floured work surface and knead briefly.

4. Divide the dough in two and wrap each in clingfilm (plastic wrap). Chill for 20 minutes.

Also try this...

~ If it's blackberry-picking time, throw in a handful on top of the apple mixture.

~ If you prefer a slightly tarter filling, use just 50g/1¾oz/¼ cup sugar.

5. Put the apples into a large pan with the sugar and cloves.

6. Drizzle over 2 tbsp cold water, cover and cook for around 10 minutes. If there's excess liquid, drain this off. Cool. Preheat the oven to 200°C/180°C fan/400°F/gas mark 6. Put a baking sheet in the oven to heat up.

7. Unwrap half the dough and roll out on a clean, lightly floured work surface until it's around 3mm/⅛in thick and is big enough to line a 24cm/9½in pie plate, leaving a little hanging over the edge. Chill while the apple cools.

8. When the apple mixture is cool, spoon the apricot jam into the pastry case and brush all over it. Fill with the apple, then brush the edge with beaten egg. Roll out the other piece of dough until large enough to cover the top and edge. Put this on top of the apple and use a knife to cut around the edge to remove any excess.

Crimp the edges then brush more beaten egg over the top and sprinkle with caster (superfine) sugar. Cook on the baking sheet for 30 minutes until golden. Serve.

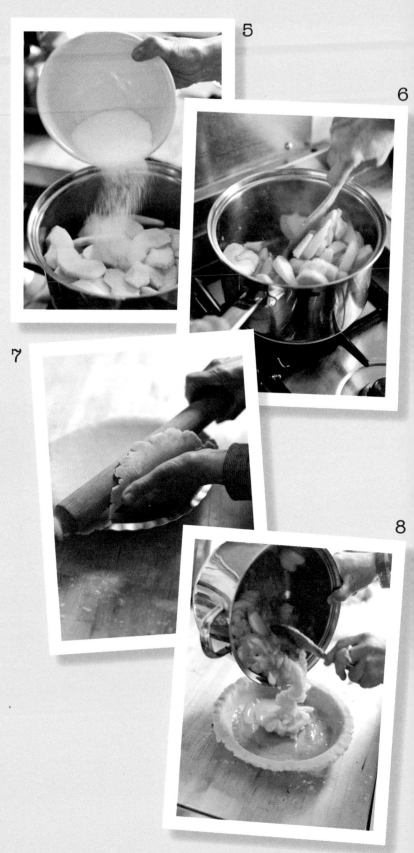

Banana splits

As much as this recipe can be an assembly job, it comes into its own when you prepare all the elements from scratch. The ice cream is the classic Italian *fior di latte*, and although you have to make this ahead, it's worth it. It's milky, melting and beautifully light. The chocolate sauce can be done in the microwave, then there's just the banana to split and nuts to chop and toast. See – it's easy!

Prep: 25 minutes, plus freezing
Cook: 5-10 minutes
Serves 4

4 bananas
100ml/3½fl oz/scant ½ cup double (heavy)
  cream, lightly whipped
40g/1½oz flaked almonds, roughly chopped
  and toasted

For the ice cream
200ml/7fl oz/scant 1 cup double (heavy)
  cream
200ml/7fl oz/scant 1 cup milk
140g/5oz/scant ¾ cup golden caster
  (superfine) sugar

For the chocolate sauce
100g/3½oz dark chocolate, broken into
  pieces
1 tbsp golden (light corn) syrup
5 tbsp single (light) cream

Make the ice cream: stir together the double (heavy) cream, milk and sugar. Churn in an ice cream machine until firm, then freeze (alternatively, pour into a shallow freezerproof container, put in the freezer, and stir every hour or so until the mixture is solid).

Make the chocolate sauce: put the chocolate, syrup and cream in a bowl and microwave on low for 5 minutes, checking halfway through, until the chocolate has melted, then stir gently. (Alternatively, if you don't have a microwave, put in a pan and melt over a low heat, stirring.)

Peel the bananas and split down the length of each one. Put in a bowl and place 2 scoops of ice cream in each split banana. Drizzle over the chocolate sauce, add a spoonful of whipped cream, scatter over some toasted chopped almonds and dig right in.

Chocolate panettone pudding

This is essentially an assembly job that can be done very quickly. It uses such rich ingredients that the result tastes as if a huge amount of time and effort has gone into it. It's great for using up that panettone you're always left with after Christmas. The diet will have to wait!

Prep: 10 minutes
Cook: 25-30 minutes
Serves 4

A little butter, for greasing
200g/7oz chocolate panettone
400ml/14fl oz/1¾ cups milk
200ml/7fl oz/scant 1 cup double
    (heavy) cream
3 medium egg yolks, plus 2 whole eggs
2 tbsp rum or brandy
Finely grated zest of 1 unwaxed orange
100g/3½oz/½ cup golden caster
    (superfine) sugar
Plain yogurt, to serve

Heat the oven to 200°C/180°C fan/400°F/ gas mark 6. Grease a 1.3ltr/2¼pt/good 3pt shallow ovenproof dish.

Cut the panettone into 1cm/½in thick slices and lay them overlapping in the dish.

Put the remaining ingredients apart from the yogurt into a large bowl and whisk everything together. Pour over the panettone, then bake for 25-30 minutes – the custard should still have a bit of a wobble in the middle.

Cool a little and serve warm with some plain yogurt to cut through the richness.

Clever cooking

~ If yours is the plain or fruity panettone, just finely chop 25g/1oz good dark chocolate and tuck the pieces in among the bread.

Love your leftovers

~ If you don't know what to do with the egg whites left over from this recipe, check out my recipe for meringues on page 204.

My winning 'F-Word' trifle

I couldn't believe it when I beat Gordon Ramsay on The F-Word with this. If you have any leftover sponge cake, you can use that instead of trifle sponges.

Prep: 30 minutes
Cook: 10 minutes
Serves 4-6

For the topping
Vegetable oil
25g/1oz flaked almonds
35g/1¼oz/generous ¼ cup golden icing
   (confectioners') sugar, plus 1 extra tbsp
450ml/16fl oz/2 cups double (heavy) cream

For the custard
300ml/10fl oz/1¼ cups single (light) cream
1 vanilla pod, split lengthways
4 medium egg yolks
50g/1¾oz/¼ cup golden caster
   (superfine) sugar

For the base
4 trifle sponges
Raspberry jam
150g/5½oz raspberries
1 large banana, sliced
2-3 tbsp sweet sherry

Preheat the oven to 200°C/180°C fan/400°F/ gas mark 6. Line a baking sheet with foil and brush with vegetable oil.

Put the flaked almonds into a sieve and rinse under cold water. Tip into a bowl and mix with the icing (confectioners') sugar. Spread out on the foil and bake in the oven for 10 minutes until caramelized. Cool.

Make the custard: pour the single (light) cream into a small pan and add the vanilla pod. Bring it just to the boil – it's ready when small bubbles appear on the edge. Remove the pod. Beat together the egg yolks and sugar, then gradually pour the cream on top, stirring all the time. Rinse out the pan, then return the mixture to the pan and heat gently until it has thickened and coats the back of the spoon. Set aside to cool a little.

Slice the trifle sponges through the middle and spread each base with jam. Put back together and use to line a trifle bowl. Sprinkle over the raspberries and banana, then douse everything in the sherry.

Spoon the custard over the top, then chill until cold. Pour the double (heavy) cream into a bowl and add the remaining tbsp of icing (confectioners') sugar. Whip just until it's still soft and floppy. Spoon on top of the custard. Break up the caramelized almonds and scatter over the top.

Love your leftovers

~ The recipe for the caramelized almonds makes slightly more than you need. Put the rest in an airtight container and enjoy within a week.

Irresistible meringues with sweet coffee and pecan cream

I've yet to serve these to anyone who hasn't come back for seconds. I like to use unrefined sugar for meringues, as it gives a rounded, more mellow flavour. It takes a little bit more time to dissolve into the meringue, but it's really worth it. You just need to be patient and whisk for a bit longer.

Prep: 10 minutes
Cook: 1½ hours, plus overnight
Serves 4

For the meringues
50g/1¾oz egg whites
100g/3½oz/½ cup golden caster
    (superfine) sugar

For the filling
300ml/10fl oz/1¼ cups double
    (heavy) cream
1 tbsp Camp coffee essence or 1 tsp coffee
    granules mixed with 1 tbsp cold water
1-2 tbsp soft light brown sugar
1 tbsp rum (optional)
25g/1oz pecans, chopped and toasted

Clever cooking

~ I always seem to have loads of egg whites in the freezer and love making meringues. I just weigh out the whites and then weigh out double the quantity of sugar.

Preheat the oven to 140°C/120°C fan/275°F/ gas mark 1. Line two baking sheets with baking parchment or a silicone sheet.

For the meringues, put the egg whites in a clean, grease-free bowl and whisk until stiff peaks form. When ready, the mixture will stick to the bowl and you should be able to hold the bowl upside down without it falling out. Add the sugar, one heaped spoonful at a time, and whisk in, making sure each spoonful has dissolved before adding another.

Blob a tiny bit of meringue on each corner of each baking sheet and stick down the parchment. Now take 2 dessertspoons and spoon about eight even-sized blobs, spaced out, on the sheet. Bake in the oven for 1½ hours, until they peel away easily from the parchment. Turn off the oven and leave the meringues in there to cool overnight.

For the filling, whisk the cream in a bowl until soft peaks form. Slowly whisk in the coffee, sugar and rum (if using) until thick. Fold in the nuts, reserving a few for serving, then sandwich the meringues together with the cream. Put on to plates and sprinkle over the remaining chopped nuts.

Spot-on gooey brownies

My friend Fiona gave me this recipe about 20 years ago, when our children were babies. This is the first time I've seen this recipe in grams. Everyone loves a brownie, which is why I always make double and freeze half. Thawing takes hardly any time. Just bring them out of the freezer about half an hour before you want to eat them.

Prep: 10 minutes
Cook: 20 minutes
Makes around 32 very rich squares

125g/4½oz/1 generous stick butter,
   plus extra for greasing
125g/4½oz good dark chocolate
3 large eggs
300g/10½oz/1½ cups soft light brown sugar
2 tsp vanilla extract
150g/5½oz/1 generous cup self-raising flour
25g/1oz cocoa powder
125g/4oz pecans or walnuts,
   toasted and roughly chopped

Clever cooking

~ It's crucial not to overbake these – the gooeyness is the whole point. You need to have the confidence to remove them from the oven almost before you think they're ready.

To freeze

~ To freeze, keep the brownie in any baking parchment that you've cooked it in. Wrap the whole thing in clingfilm (plastic wrap) and freeze for up to one month. To thaw, take the packet out of the freezer and unwrap half an hour before you want to eat them.

Preheat the oven to 180°C/160°C fan/350°F/gas mark 4.

Put the butter and chocolate in a heatproof bowl and melt on low in a microwave, checking it every couple of minutes. (Alternatively, put it over a pan of simmering water, making sure the base doesn't touch the water, and allow it to melt slowly.) Stir the two ingredients together, then set aside to cool a little.

Grease and line a 16 x 26cm/6¼ x 10½in baking tin with baking parchment.

Whisk the eggs, sugar and vanilla extract in a bowl until thick and moussey. When you lift the whisk out of the bowl, it should leave a ribbon-like trail.

Sift the flour and cocoa over the mousse mixture, then pour the chocolate mixture carefully around it. Add the nuts. Use a large metal spoon to fold everything together. You can be gentle at first, so as not to knock out too much air, but towards the end use firm, fast strokes.

Pour into the prepared tin and bake for 20 minutes.

Cool in the tin. Lift out and cut into squares.

Bits and pieces that make life so much better

Bits and pieces that make life so much better

No-need-to-rise fruity soda bread

This easy loaf can be on the table within the hour. It's based on Irish soda bread, but flavoured with fruit and herbs. Instead of using buttermilk, which can be hard to get hold of, I've used plain yogurt. You don't need to knead the dough – just work it enough to bring all the ingredients together to make it smooth.

Prep: 10 minutes
Cook: 45-50 minutes
Makes 1 loaf

600g/1lb 5oz/4¼ cups plain
   (all-purpose) flour
1½ tsp baking powder
1 tsp salt
1 sprig fresh rosemary, finely chopped
75g/2¾oz/scant ½ cup sultanas
   (golden raisins)
500g/1lb 2oz plain yogurt (not thick set)

Preheat the oven to 220°C/200°C fan/ 425°F/gas mark 7. Line a baking sheet with baking parchment.

Sift the flour and baking powder into a bowl. Stir in the salt, rosemary and sultanas (golden raisins). Make a well in the centre and stir in the yogurt. (I find it easy to do this bit with a round-bladed table knife.)

Tip the mixture on to a board and knead quickly and evenly until smooth. Flatten into a 17cm/6½in round, and slide on to the baking sheet. Push a wooden spoon handle vertically down on the middle and then across it, until the loaf measures around 20cm/8in across.

Bake in the oven for 20 minutes, then reduce the oven temperature to 200°C/180°C fan/400°F/gas mark 6, and bake for a further 25-30 minutes, or until the loaf sounds hollow when tapped on the bottom.

Cool slightly on a wire rack – this bread is best eaten warm.

Moist and nutty banana bread

The secret to a flavoursome, fruity banana bread is black-spotted bananas that are just on the turn. Yellow ones simply don't cut it. You can also freeze them whole in their skins. When thawed, they'll be delightfully mushy inside.

Prep: 15 minutes
Cook: 1 hour
Makes 1 large loaf

125g/4½oz/generous stick butter, melted and cooled, plus extra to grease
350g/12oz/2½ cups self-raising flour
175g/6oz/scant cup golden caster (superfine) sugar
75g/2¾oz walnuts, roughly chopped
A good grating of nutmeg
2 medium eggs, beaten
3 large overripe bananas, peeled and mashed
A dash of milk

Preheat the oven to 190°C/170°C fan/375°F/gas mark 5. Grease and line a 900g/2lb loaf tin with baking parchment so it comes 5cm/2in higher than the edge of the tin.

Sift the flour into a bowl. Add the sugar, nuts and nutmeg. Make a well in the centre and add the butter, eggs and bananas, then mix everything together. Drizzle over a little milk if the mixture is on the dry side, and stir again.

Spoon into the prepared tin and bake for 1 hour, or until a metal skewer inserted into the loaf comes out clean.

Cool on a wire rack, then slice.

To freeze
~ This keeps well in an airtight container for up to five days, or freeze for up to a month wrapped well in clingfilm (plastic wrap).

Auntie Hughag's Scotch pancakes

My Auntie Hughag (short for Hughina) is the most amazing baker. All her grandchildren are boys, and I hope they know how lucky they are having unlimited access to permanently packed tins of homemade cakes and biscuits. Her Scotch pancakes are sublime. The mixture will be a little thin, but it thickens slightly as the flour starts to expand, and makes them lovely and light.

Prep: 5 minutes
Cook: around 15 minutes
Makes around 30 pancakes

15g/½oz butter, plus extra for frying
1 tbsp golden syrup (light corn syrup)
125g/4½oz/scant cup self-raising flour
¼ tsp each bicarbonate of soda
   (baking soda) and cream of tartar
A pinch of salt
2 tbsp golden caster (superfine) sugar
1 medium egg
200ml/7fl oz/scant cup milk

Melt the butter and syrup in a small dish in the microwave on low or in a very small pan. Sift the flour into a large bowl. Stir in the bicarbonate of soda (baking soda), cream of tartar, salt and sugar. Make a well in the centre and add the egg. Beat a little to mix roughly, then slowly pour in the milk,
stirring to combine. Don't worry if there's a few small lumps in there still, it won't matter. Stir in the butter and syrup mixture.

Heat a flat griddle or frying pan (skillet) until hot. Add a little butter and when melted, drop 3 separate tbsp of the mixture on to the pan. When the surface bubbles, turn with a palette knife and cook until nicely browned. Continue in this way with the rest of the mixture.

Cool on a wire rack and eat with butter and jam.

Granny's scones

These are legendary. My mother's mother made them almost daily (bread was a once-a-week delivery in the remote north-west of Scotland) and they were eaten with crowdie, which is a cream cheese that's sharp and dense. My mother does these too, and they are the talk of the area. And of course it's the recipe I always use. A few ingredients to get together, sure, but my goodness the results are unbeatable.

Prep: 15 minutes
Cook: around 10 minutes
Makes 16 scones

40g/1½oz/3 tbsp butter
1 level tbsp golden (light corn) syrup
1 medium egg
300ml/10fl oz/1¼ cups buttermilk
   (if you can get it) or milk
450g/1lb/3¼ cups plain (all-purpose) flour
1 tsp bicarbonate of soda (baking soda)
1 heaped tsp cream of tartar
1 heaped tsp salt

Preheat the oven to the hottest setting and place a large baking sheet inside.

Melt the butter and syrup together in a pan. Mix the egg and buttermilk together. Put the dry ingredients in a large bowl. Add both the wet mixtures to the dry ingredients and stir with a large metal spoon. (If you use milk instead of buttermilk, the mix might seem too wet but fear not.)

Have lots of flour on your work surface and empty the mix on to it. Sprinkle on a good layer of flour. Gently roll out into a rough circle about 2cm/¾in thick. Cut up into 16 pieces; some will be square, some will be corners, but they'll all taste gorgeous.

Arrange on the hot baking sheet (no need to grease) in the round shape, spaced a little apart. Put in the oven for about 7-8 minutes until nicely golden. Cool on a wire rack.

My mum's award-winning shortbread

So called because whenever there was a country show when we were growing up, my mum would always be asked to enter her bakes for the competitions. The shortbread won first prize every time. The trick is to shape it, leaving a gap between the edge and the rim of the tin, then bake until it's golden, taking it as far as you can without over-browning.

Prep: 10 minutes
Cook: 40 minutes
Makes 16 pieces

200g/7oz/scant 1½ cups plain (all-purpose) flour, sifted, plus extra for rolling out
50g/1¾oz/⅓ cup cornflour, sifted
175g/6oz/1½ sticks butter, softened and diced
75g/2¾oz/scant ½ cup golden caster (superfine) sugar, plus extra to sprinkle

Preheat the oven to 170°C/150°C fan/325°F/gas mark 3.

Put both flours, the butter and sugar into a food processor and whiz until the ingredients come together to make a soft dough.

Divide the mixture in half and roll one piece out on a clean, lightly floured work surface into a round measuring 16cm/6¼in in diameter. Lift into an 18 or 20cm/7 or 8in round non-stick sandwich tin and press a fork along the edges. Prick all over with the fork right through to the tin. Do the same with the other round in a separate tin.

Bake both tins in the oven for 40 minutes.

Take out of the oven and mark into triangles straightaway. Sprinkle with sugar, then leave in the tins to cool.

Storage
~ Store in an airtight container for up to five days – if they don't go as soon as you've baked them!

Scottish morning rolls

I've been making this recipe for a while, and I have perfected the exact balance of ingredients. There's a lot of liquid, but this is one of the reasons why these rolls are lovely and light. I discovered that using plain flour, as opposed to strong bread flour, gives a light crumb and soft outer crust. These rolls are lovely with butter and marmalade or use them for a special bacon and egg breakfast.

Prep: 15 minutes, plus rising and proving time
Cook: 20 minutes
Makes 8 rolls

450g/1lb/3¼ cups plain (all-purpose) flour
1 tsp fast-action dried (active dry) yeast
2 tsp salt
350ml/12fl oz/1½ cups lukewarm milk

To freeze

~ Wrap well in clingfilm (plastic wrap) and freeze for up to three months. When you're ready to eat them, take out of the freezer and thaw overnight.

Sift the flour into a large bowl and stir in the yeast and salt. Make a well in the centre and pour in the milk. Use a knife to mix well to make a soft, sticky mixture. (You can also carry out this stage in a free-standing mixer with a dough hook.) Cover and leave to rise for 40 minutes in a warm place.

Tip out of the bowl on to a lightly floured surface and divide into eight pieces. Roll each one lightly into a round and place on a floured baking sheet or one that's lined with baking parchment. Place a little bit apart so each one can prove into the next. Leave for 20 minutes.

Preheat the oven to 190°C/170°C fan/375°F/ gas mark 5.

Bake the rolls in the oven for 20 minutes, or until they sound hollow when tapped underneath.

Crumbly oatcakes

My Sutherland granny made the best oatcakes ever, and while my younger sister was working in the area she got this recipe from a local domestic science teacher. They remind me of Granny's, are a million times tastier than bought, and are easier than you think to make.

Prep: 20 minutes
Cook: 20-25 minutes
Makes 20-22

75g/2¾oz/⅔ stick butter, softened,
   plus extra to grease
225g/8oz/2⅔ cups oatmeal,
   plus extra to dust
125g/4½oz/scant cup self-raising flour
½ tsp bicarbonate of soda (baking soda)
½ tsp salt
1 tbsp milk

Preheat the oven to 180°C/160°C fan/ 350°F/gas mark 4. Lightly butter two baking sheets.

Put the dry ingredients into a bowl, then add the butter and rub in. Add the milk and 3 tbsp cold water and stir in. Bring the mixture together with your hands to make a dough.

Sprinkle some oatmeal over a clean work surface and roll out half the dough until it is about 2mm/¹⁄₁₆in thick into a vaguely round shape. Cut into triangles.

Using a palette knife, place on the baking sheets and bake for 20-25 minutes. Cool on a wire rack and store in an airtight container for up to three days.

Also try this...
~ These are just as gorgeous with a good chunk of cheese and chutney as they are on their own with a cup of tea in the afternoon.
~ For a sweet oatcake, stir 1 tbsp sugar into the oatmeal and flour mixture.

Quick raspberry jam

This is what I make from the rich pickings of my allotment every year. If you're new to jam-making, you don't need any special equipment, just a medium pan.

Prep: 5 minutes
Cook: 10 minutes
Makes about 600g/1lb 5 oz

300g/10½oz raspberries
300g/10½oz/1½ cups granulated (regular)
   sugar
A little butter

Put two saucers in the freezer to chill quickly.

Tip the raspberries into a preserving pan or large pan. Place over a high heat and then bring to the boil, stirring. Cook until the fruit is bubbling.

Whip the pan off the heat and add the sugar. Stir in and it will dissolve immediately. Bring to a rolling boil and cook for 4 minutes only.

Take the pan off the heat and put a spoonful on to a chilled saucer. Return to the freezer for 1 minute. Take out and push your finger through it – it's ready to pot when it wrinkles. If it doesn't wrinkle, continue to cook, checking every minute.

Pot in sterilized jars (see tip on page 226), seal and label.

My pressure-cooker marmalade

Using a pressure cooker halves the time it takes to make this seasonal preserve. You just pop the fruit in whole, then it's butter-soft and easy to slice once cooked.

Prep: 30 minutes
Cook: 40 minutes
Makes around 1.2kg/2¾lb

4 Seville oranges (500g/1lb 2oz total weight)
1 lemon
1kg/2¼lb/5 cups granulated (regular) sugar

Storage

~ The marmalade is ready to eat straightaway, or will keep happily in a cool dark place for up to a year.

Clever cooking

~ To sterilize jars in the oven, preheat the oven to 140°C/120°C fan/275°F/gas mark 1. Wash and rinse the jars, then turn them upside down and place on a baking sheet in the oven until dry – approximately 15 minutes.

Put the Seville oranges into a pressure cooker with the lemon. Pour in 1.1 ltr/scant 2pt/scant 5 cups cold water. Secure the lid, bring up to high pressure and cook for 20 minutes. Let out the steam, then open the lid and cool.

Halve the oranges around the equator and use a spoon to scoop out the insides into a sieve resting over a bowl. Do the same with the lemon.

Work the mixture back and forth in the sieve with a wooden spoon to extract as much purée as possible. Tip into a preserving, or very large, pan with the water from the pressure cooker.

Put the orange shells in pairs inside each other and slice finely to the thickness of your liking. Pop these into the preserving pan, too.

Put a couple of saucers in the freezer to chill quickly.

Bring the mixture up to the boil. Quickly take the pan off the heat and then stir in the sugar – it should dissolve immediately in the heat of the liquid. Return the pan to the heat and bring up to a rolling boil. Cook for at least 10 minutes.

To test for a set, take the pan off the heat and put a spoonful of the mixture on to a chilled saucer. Return to the freezer for about a minute to cool quickly. Run your finger through the middle – if it wrinkles, it's ready to pot. If not, continue to boil, checking every 2-3 minutes.

Pot into sterilized jars, cover and label.

Butter-rich lemon curd

I love this on hot toast or in the middle of a Victoria sponge. It needs to be chilled straightaway and, because it's made with butter and eggs, enjoyed within a week once opened.

Prep: 10 minutes
Cook: 15 minutes
Makes 225g/8oz

Juice of 2 lemons – around 100ml/3½fl oz/
    scant ½ cup
2 medium eggs, beaten
60g/2¼oz/¼ cup granulated (regular) sugar
60g/2¼oz/generous ½ stick butter,
    chopped and chilled

Put everything into a bowl and place over a pan of simmering water, making sure the base doesn't touch the water. Cook slowly, stirring often, until the mixture turns thick and opaque.

Strain through a sieve and pot into a sterilized jar (see tip opposite).

Clever cooking

~ If you like really citrusy curd, add the finely grated zest of one of the lemons.

Best of summer berry compote

This recipe transforms all those gorgeous summer berries into a glamorous pud and it's also a canny way to rejuvenate any pieces that have gone soft and squashy in the punnet. It's delicious with ice cream, a spoonful of thick Greek yogurt, or over meringues and whipped cream.

Prep: 10 minutes
Cook: 10 minutes
Serves 4

150g/5½oz each of raspberries
    and blueberries
Juice of 1 orange
1 tbsp golden caster (superfine) sugar
400g/14oz strawberries

Put half the raspberries and blueberries in a pan with the orange juice and sugar. Bring to the boil and simmer for 3-4 minutes, until saucy.

While the fruit is cooking, put the remaining raspberries and blueberries in a serving bowl. Add the strawberries, halved or quartered if large.

Strain the raspberry and blueberry mixture through a sieve resting over a bowl, pushing the mixture back and forth with a wooden spoon to extract as much juice as possible. Pour over the fruit in the dish and serve straightaway.

Make ahead

~ You can make the compote up to three days ahead. Store in an airtight container and chill.

Heavenly onion jam

This is really rich but I think it's the best spread for a steak and ciabatta sandwich or a chicken and bacon roll. Because it's made with butter, it won't last as long as a fruit jam, so keep it in the fridge and eat within two weeks.

Prep: 15 minutes
Cook: 1½ hours
Makes 550g/1¼lb

1kg/2¼lb onions, sliced
150g/5½oz/1¼ sticks butter
2 tsp salt
175g/6oz/scant cup golden caster
   (superfine) sugar
175ml/6fl oz/¾ cup red wine vinegar
300ml/10fl oz/1¼ cups red wine

Put the onions in a pan with the butter and salt. Cover and cook gently over a low heat, stirring every now and then, for about 20 minutes, until softened. It may look as if there isn't enough butter, but once it has melted, the onions will soon start to reduce and cook down.

Add the sugar, turn up the heat slightly and bubble, uncovered, for about 20 minutes, until the onions start to look a bit fudgey, stirring the mixture often.

Pour the vinegar and red wine over the mixture and bring to the boil. Simmer for around 50 minutes over a low heat, again stirring often, until the onions are soft and jammy.

Pot into sterilized jars (see page 226) and leave to cool before storing in the fridge.

clever cooking

~ Although I love prepping veg, I draw the line at chopping lots of onions, so I use the slicer attachment on my food processor for this.

Liz's rich chocolate praline

I've eaten a ton of this over the years. It's my dear friend Liz's signature occasion offering: a heavenly combination of smashed-up biscuits and other yummy goodies that's addictive. Liz doesn't include raisins – they're just my way of lessening the guilt that's inevitably induced.

Prep: 20 minutes
Cook: 5 minutes
Makes 25 very moreish squares

125g/4½oz/generous stick butter, plus extra
   for greasing
2 tbsp golden (light corn) syrup
3 tbsp cocoa powder (unsweetened cocoa)
A handful of raisins
21 McVitie's digestive biscuits
   (Graham crackers), crushed
   but not pulverized
200g/7oz dark chocolate (minimum
   50% cocoa solids), broken into pieces

Grease a 26 x 16cm/10½ x 6¼in cake tin.

Put the rest of the butter in a medium pan with the syrup and cocoa. Melt, then remove from the heat and add the raisins and crushed biscuits. Stir it all together then spoon into the tin.

Melt the dark chocolate (see below) and pour it over the top, tilting the tin around so it runs into the sides and corners. Chill for about 30 minutes, then cut into pieces before the mixture goes hard.

Chill for another hour or so, then remove from tin and enjoy. Wrap in clingfilm (plastic wrap), and keep in the fridge for up to a week.

clever cooking

~ You can melt the chocolate in the microwave, but be very, very careful you don't burn it. Cook on low for 1-2 minutes at a time. Otherwise put into a heatproof bowl and set over a pan of simmering water for a few minutes (make sure the bowl doesn't touch the water), giving it a little stir with a fork now and then.

Gone-in-a-flash tablet

Tablet, a sort of hard fudge, is Scotland's national sweet. Everyone loves it – and has the fillings to prove it. There are lots of commercial brands but I've yet to taste one that meets homemade standards. Little packs used to be sold at sales of work in small villages where I grew up…you had to check with the person taking the money which tablet was made by whom (you always had to be there at the beginning to get some made by Mrs Garrow the Dell). It's tricky to make, and it needs to be crumbly but not grainy, but after a couple of tries you'll be hooked (my sis Karen is now an expert).

Prep: 5 minutes
Cook: 1 hour
Makes 40 pieces

125g/4½oz/generous stick butter,
    plus extra to grease
1kg/2¼lb/5 cups granulated sugar
300ml/10fl oz/1¼ cups full-fat milk
200g/7oz condensed milk
2 tsp vanilla extract

Love your leftovers

~ Store any leftovers in an airtight container. It'll be just as delicious in a few days though the texture will dry out slightly.

Clever cooking

~ If you have a jam thermometer, you can use that to keep an eye on the mixture when it's boiling to the soft ball stage, which is 116°C/241°F, although you'll still need to test it in a bowl of cold water.

Grease a 23 x 33cm/9 x 13in tin with butter.

Melt the butter, sugar and milk in a pan over a low heat. Allow the sugar to dissolve completely. This is a really important stage and will take around half an hour. To check the sugar has completely dissolved, dip a large spoon into the mixture and lift it out. Leave until cool enough to run your finger through it – it's ready when you can't feel any grains.

Bring the mixture to the boil and cook for 10 minutes, stirring occasionally. Add the condensed milk, then continue to simmer for another 10 minutes on a slightly lower heat, stirring all the time. Keep cooking until the mixture reaches 'soft ball' stage. To test this, spoon a little of the mixture into a bowl of ice-cold water; when it forms a soft ball, it's ready.

Remove the pan from the heat and add the vanilla. Beat the mixture really well and constantly for 3-5 minutes, until it thickens. This stage is very important.

Pour into the prepared tin and leave to set. When cold, cut into squares.

Elderflower cordial

Making this fragrant drink is an annual Ewan/Aggie ritual in May. There are countless elder trees on the allotments behind our house, and I love gathering the pretty cream-coloured blossoms. Better to get the flowers before they're too far gone (usually by the end of May, though slightly later in cooler parts). You can turn out gallons of this stuff for very little money or effort – and it's lovely to give away. I collect an assortment of little bottles whenever I remember throughout the year. Scary amounts of sugar, indeed, but remember it's well diluted. Just add ice and sparkling water or, for a more grown-up tipple, prosecco or sparkling wine. A drizzle is good in a gooseberry fool or over vanilla ice cream.

Prep: 30 minutes
Cook: 10 minutes, plus steeping time
Makes 2ltr/3½pt/8 cups

20 elderflower heads
2 unwaxed lemons
2kg/4½lb/10 cups golden granulated sugar
80g/scant 3oz citric acid

Pour 1.14 ltr/2pt/4 cups water into a pan, cover and bring to the boil.

Shake the elderflower heads into the sink to set free any bugs. Pare the lemon peel and slice the fruit.

Take the pan off the heat, stir in the sugar then pour the mixture into a large bowl. Stir in the citric acid, then add the elderflower heads, lemon peel and slices. Set aside for at least 12 hours.

Strain through spotlessly clean muslin, then pour into sterilized bottles (see tip, left) and seal. This will keep in the fridge for several months.

clever cooking

~ To sterilize the bottles, wash well in hot soapy water, then rinse. Put the bottles and stoppers in an empty sink and fill with boiling water, allowing it to run over the edges and flow over the stopper. Pour the boiling water away and use a sterilized funnel to fill the bottle with the cordial. Seal immediately.

Savoury rice

Here's a quick and easy way of making rice more interesting. It may look like a long list of ingredients for something so simple, but they're all the storecupboard bits I make sure I always have in. It's lovely with a pork chop or some leftover roast chicken stirred in.

Prep: 10 minutes
Cook: 20 minutes
Serves 4

1 tbsp olive or vegetable oil
1 onion, finely chopped
1 celery stick (if you have it), finely chopped
1 garlic clove, sliced
250g/9oz/1⅓ cups long-grain rice
500ml/18fl oz/2¼ cups hot vegetable stock
1 bay leaf
A sprig of thyme
Salt and freshly ground black pepper

Heat the oil in a medium pan. Fry the onion and celery over a medium heat for 5-8 minutes, until the onion starts to turn golden. Add the garlic and cook for 1 minute.

Stir in the rice, then pour over the hot stock and add the bay and thyme. Season well. Cover, bring to the boil, then turn the heat down low. The rice will be ready when all the water has been absorbed.

Fluff up with a fork and serve.

Great for kids

~ This is a great dish for bumping up the vegetable quota for kids. A peeled chopped stalk of broccoli works well – add it with the garlic. Or you could try stirring in a couple of spoonfuls of thawed frozen peas right at the end.

Easy-peasy tomato sauce

This recipe's a great way to get ahead with one of the midweek meals. It's a basic tomato sauce that you can cook in the oven at the same time as the Sunday roast. No need to sauté the onions – just put it all in the pan and let the oven do the work. Serve with pasta, or purée it and spoon it over fish, throw in some olives and cook in the oven.

Prep: 10 minutes
Cook: 1-2 hours
Serves 4

1 tbsp olive oil
1 garlic clove, sliced
1 onion, finely chopped
1 carrot, finely chopped
1 celery stick, finely chopped
400g/14oz canned chopped tomatoes
400ml/14fl oz/1¾ cups hot chicken
   or vegetable stock
1 bay leaf
A pinch of granulated (regular) sugar
1 scant tsp balsamic vinegar

Preheat the oven to 190°C/170°C/375°F/ gas mark 5.

Put all the ingredients, apart from the vinegar, in an ovenproof casserole pan and place in the oven. Cook for 1-2 hours, stirring every now and then.

Stir in the vinegar and whip out and discard the bay leaf. Leave to cool, then purée if you like.

To freeze
~ Once cool, scrape into a container and chill for up to three days or freeze for up to a month.

Hilary's millionaire's shortbread

Hilary, my cousin's lovely ex-wife, is a great baker. I first tasted this about 20 years ago, thought it was the best ever (millionaire's shortbread is a national addiction), and she happily gave me the recipe. I've been making it ever since.

Prep time: 30 minutes
Cooking time: 40 minutes
Makes 32 squares

For the shortbread
200g/7oz/scant 1½ cups plain (all-purpose) flour
50g/1¾oz/⅓ cup cornflour (cornstarch)
175g/6oz/1½ sticks butter, softened
75g/2¾oz/scant ½ cup golden caster (superfine) sugar

For the caramel
175g/6oz condensed milk
125g/4½oz/generous stick butter
50g/1¾oz/¼ cup soft brown sugar
2 tbsp golden (light corn) syrup

For the topping
75g/2¾oz each plain chocolate and milk chocolate, broken into squares

Preheat the oven to 170°C/150°C fan/325°F/gas mark 3.

Put both flours, the butter and sugar into a food processor and whiz until the ingredients come together to make a soft dough. Tip on to a clean work surface dusted with a little extra flour and bring together with your hands.

Roll out to roughly fit a shallow baking tin with a base measurement of 26 x 16cm/10½ x 6¼in. Lift the dough into the tin, then use the back of a spoon to edge it into the corners and to level the surface. Prick all over with a fork and bake for 40 minutes. Remove from the oven and set aside.

Make the caramel. Put the ingredients in a pan and place over a low heat to melt the butter. Bring gently to the boil, stirring all the time, then reduce the heat to a simmer and cook for 7 minutes only. You may get a few brown spots where the sugar has caramelized but this isn't a problem – it will only enhance the flavour.

Use a spatula to scrape all the golden goo over the shortbread base in the tin, covering it completely. Allow to cool.

Melt the chocolate in a bowl over a pan of simmering water, making sure the base doesn't touch the water. (You can also do this in the microwave on the lowest heat setting, checking it every few minutes.) Spoon the melted chocolate over the caramel, using a spatula to cover it evenly, and allow to cool.

Cut into squares and try to resist making a pig of yourself.

Meatloaf that hits the spot

There's very little prep with this one, as the food processor is your friend here. Put everything in, following the order below, and there's no need to wash the bowl between takes. It's a great family meal served hot with a baked potato and a salad alongside, and is also good sliced thinly on a sandwich with a gutsy chutney.

Prep: 20 minutes
Cook: 1 hour 30 minutes
**Serves 4, with plenty of leftovers
   for lunch**

4 slices day-old white or brown bread,
   crusts removed
1 small onion, roughly chopped
½ green (bell) pepper, roughly chopped
450g/1lb pork tenderloin, sliced
2-3 sprigs each of fresh sage and thyme
500g/1lb 2oz sausagemeat or sausages
   (made with minimum 90% pork)
1 tsp salt
½ tsp each of cayenne pepper and
   ground white pepper
1 tbsp tomato ketchup
1-2 dashes Worcestershire sauce
1 medium egg
Vegetable oil, for greasing

To freeze

~ Wrap whatever's left in clingfilm (plastic wrap) or foil and it'll taste just as good up to three days later. Or freeze for up to a month. Thaw overnight and use immediately.

Preheat the oven to 170°C/150°C fan/325°F/ gas mark 3. Line the base of a 900g/2lb loaf tin with baking parchment.

Put the bread in a food processor and whiz to make breadcrumbs. Tip into a large bowl. Put the onion and green pepper in the processor and whiz to chop finely. Add to the bowl.

Now whiz the pork and herbs until the meat is minced. Add to the bowl with the sausagemeat (or the filling squeezed out of the sausage skins), salt, cayenne, white pepper, ketchup, Worcestershire sauce and egg. Using your (clean!) hands, mix all the ingredients together well.

Spoon the mixture into the lined loaf tin and level the surface with the back of the fork. Cover the top with lightly oiled foil. Bake on a lipped baking sheet, to catch any juices, for 1½ hours.

Leave to stand in the tin for 10 minutes, then run a knife around the edge of the loaf. Turn it upside down on to a plate, slice and serve.

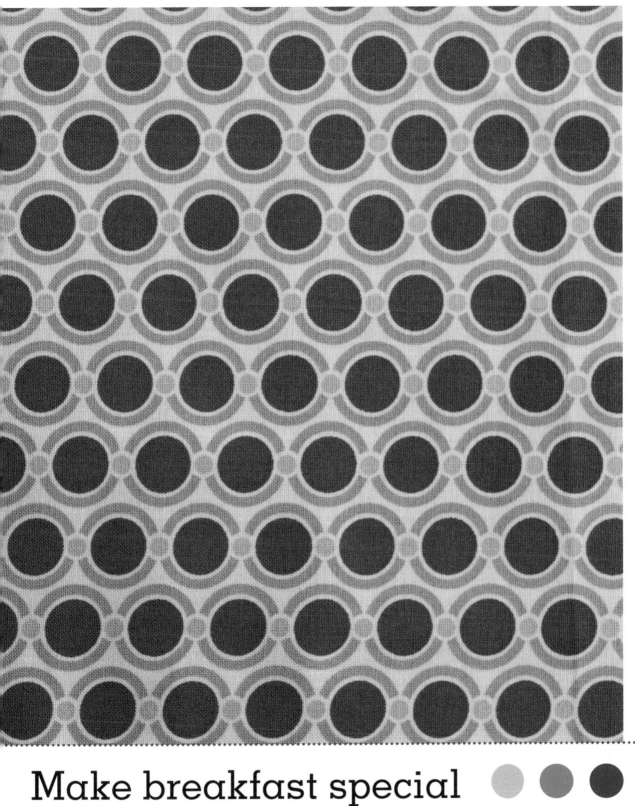

Make breakfast special

Make breakfast special

The most indulgent breakfast treat

These are a cross between a Chelsea bun and a recipe I found in one of Jamie Oliver's books. They're not too sweet, despite the chocolate spread, and I like the fact that I know exactly what's gone into them.

Prep: 30 minutes, plus rising and proving
Cook: 20-25 minutes
Makes 12 buns

350g/12oz/2½ cups strong white bread flour, plus extra for dusting
5g/⅛oz fast-action dried (active dry) yeast
1 tbsp golden caster (superfine) sugar
½ tsp salt
25g/1oz/¼ stick butter, chopped
100ml/3½fl oz/scant ½ cup milk
1 medium egg, beaten
2½ tbsp Nutella
35g/1¼oz hazelnuts, toasted and chopped
1 banana, peeled and cut into wafer-thin slices

Sift the flour into a large bowl. Stir in the yeast, 2 tsp of the sugar and the salt.

Measure 100ml/3½fl oz/scant ½ cup boiling water in a jug. Stir in the butter and allow it to melt, then add the milk. Make a well in the centre of the flour and pour in the liquid, followed by the egg. Mix with a knife to make a rough dough, then tip on to a board and knead until soft and sticky. (You can also do this in a free-standing mixer using a dough hook.) Put the dough back in the bowl, cover and leave to rise for 40 minutes.

Roll out the dough on a lightly floured surface until it measures around 28 x 35cm/ 11 x 14in. Spread the Nutella thinly over the top, sprinkle over half the hazelnuts, leaving a 5cm/2in border from the top, then do the same with the banana. Roll from the bottom up. Cut into 12 rolls and place cut side down, about 1cm/½in apart, on a baking sheet lined with baking parchment or silicone. Set aside to prove for 30 minutes.

Preheat the oven to 190°C/170°C fan/375°F/ gas mark 5. Sprinkle the remaining nuts and sugar over the top of the buns. Bake for 20-25 minutes, until evenly golden. Cool on a wire rack and serve.

Chewy bagels

I live in an area in north London that has lots of bagel shops and, once I'd tasted the real deal, was keen to make my own. My late Jewish mother-in-law was impressed.

Prep: 25 minutes, plus rising time
Cook: 35 minutes
Makes 8

500g/1lb 2oz/good 3½ cups
   strong white flour
1 tsp fast-action dried (active dry) yeast
1 tbsp granulated (regular) sugar
2 tsp salt
A little vegetable oil
1 tbsp malt extract
Cream cheese and smoked salmon
   (or raspberry jam), to serve

Sift the flour into a large bowl and stir in the yeast, sugar and salt. Stir together, then make a well in the centre. Pour in 375ml/13fl oz/good 1½ cups lukewarm water and mix with a knife to make a soft, sticky dough. (Or use a free-standing mixer to make the dough.) Knead briefly, then put back into a clean bowl. Cover and leave to rise in a warm place for 45 minutes.

Tip the dough on to a lightly floured board. Divide the dough in half, then divide each half into four pieces. Roll one piece into a rope about 18cm/7in long, then connect it at the other end to make a ring of dough. Put on a heavily floured board, and repeat to make eight rings. Cover and leave to rise in a warm place for 20 minutes.

Preheat the oven to 200°C/180°C fan/400°F/gas mark 6. Put two oiled baking sheets in the oven to preheat.

Bring a large frying pan (skillet) of water to the boil. Stir in the malt extract. When the water is bubbling, slowly lower four bagels into it and poach for 2-3 minutes on one side. Flip over and cook the other side for the same time. Lift out with a slotted spoon and place on a plate. Cook the other four in the same way. Divide the bagels between two hot baking sheets. Bake for 20 minutes, until golden, then cool on a rack. Serve with cream cheese and smoked salmon (or raspberry jam).

My dad's daily porridge

My father grew up on a farm near Aviemore, where they had porridge first and last thing every single day. He continued to have it for breakfast throughout his adult life. It was always real porridge, as he called it – made with oatmeal, water and salt and 'not those namby-pamby rolled oats slathered in syrup and allsorts'. He would pour it into an old-fashioned soup plate and have a bowl separately on the side containing half milk, half double cream and take his spoon from one to the other then to his mouth. He was a blacksmith, so calories held no fear for him.

Prep: 10 minutes
Cook: 5 minutes
Serves 4 generously

200g/7oz/scant 2½ cups oatmeal
A pinch of salt
800ml/27fl oz/scant 3½ cups boiling water
Milk, to serve
Whatever adornments you fancy, such
    as maple syrup

Put the oatmeal and salt in a pan and add just enough cold water to cover it. Allow the oats to swell for 5-10 minutes.

Pour over the boiling water and bring to the boil, stirring constantly. Turn the heat right down and cook for 5 minutes, continuing to stir.

Ladle into four bowls and serve with milk and any other adornments you fancy, such as maple syrup (my son Ewan's favourite).

Ewan's eggs Benedict

My son makes this for me every Mother's Day and it's always gorgeous. It's a pretty hands-on dish, but with rich rewards. The trick is to get everything ready – he's honed the method to the one below – then it's a last-minute assembly job.

Prep: 25 minutes
Cook: 5 minutes
Serves 4

A little oil
4 large eggs
2 muffins
4 slices good-quality ham
Snipped fresh chives for the top

For the hollandaise
1 tsp white wine vinegar
2 medium egg yolks
Salt and white pepper
100g/3½oz/scant stick butter, softened
A squeeze of lemon juice

Line a small ramekin with a large piece of clingfilm (plastic wrap), then oil it inside. Drop an egg into it. Twist the clingfilm to seal, making sure there's no air trapped inside. Twist the neck of the bundle really well – you don't want the egg leaching out when it's in the water. Repeat with the remaining eggs. Set aside until you're ready to cook them.

Split the muffins, then toast and keep them warm.

Make the hollandaise. Put the vinegar into a medium bowl with the egg yolks. Beat well and season with salt and white pepper. Rest this bowl over a pan of just-simmering water, making sure the base doesn't touch it. Cook for a minute to heat up the eggs, then add the butter in small bits, beating well after each addition. The mixture will start to thicken into a lovely, rich-coloured unctuous sauce. Keep stirring all the time. Take it off the heat if it looks like it's going to curdle.

Bring a pan of water up to a simmer. Lift the clingfilmed eggs from the ramekins, drop into the water and simmer for 3 minutes.

Divide the toasted muffins between four plates. Top with a slice of ham. When the eggs are ready, carefully take them out of the water and unwrap, putting one on each slice of ham. Coat with the hollandaise, scatter over the chives, season and serve.

Clever cooking

~ If the hollandaise sauce splits, you can rescue it. Whip the bowl out of the pan. Put another egg yolk in a clean bowl. Place this over the heat and add the curdled mixture, spoonful by spoonful, beating it in quickly and evenly. It won't take nearly as long as the first time round.

~ This is a great dish for lunch, too. Serve some spinach alongside, either wilted in a pan or in the microwave. A handful for each person will be enough.

French toast, crispy bacon and peaches

Here's something I make on many a Sunday. It's really indulgent but I reckon that's allowed at breakfast time. The maple syrup has to be the real deal – don't ever buy the cheap stuff as it tastes horrid.

Prep: 10 minutes
Cook: 10 minutes
Serves 4

8 streaky bacon rashers (strips)
3 medium eggs
A splash of milk
1 tbsp caster (superfine) sugar
4 thickish slices bloomer bread,
    crusts removed
A little butter
2 peaches, sliced
A good drizzle of maple syrup

Preheat the grill (broiler) and cook the bacon until crispy, or done to your liking.

Beat the eggs with the milk and sugar in a large shallow dish. Add two slices of bread, leave for a moment or two to soak up the eggy mixture, then turn over.

Heat a knob (pat) of butter and fry the bread until golden on one side; turn over and fry the second side. Repeat with the other two slices. (If the butter looks as if it has burned between batches, give the frying pan/skillet a wipe with a piece of kitchen paper and cook those slices with some fresh butter.)

Divide between four plates, top with the bacon and sliced peaches and drizzle over a little maple syrup. Serve extra syrup on the side.

clever cooking
~ When peaches aren't available, throw over a handful of blueberries instead.

Black pudding and egg on homemade rolls

It's really worth saving some of the rolls on page 222 for this special breakfast. I love the combination of the savoury black pudding and the fried egg's creamy yolk with that soft, fluffy bun underneath. If I'm on a (semi) health kick, I'll poach the eggs, which gives a lighter touch but is no less delicious.

Prep: 2 minutes
Cook: 10 minutes
Serves 4

A little sunflower, vegetable or olive oil
4 slices black pudding (blood sausage)
4 eggs
4 Scottish Morning Rolls (see page 212)
Salt and freshly ground black pepper

Heat a little oil in a pan and fry the black pudding (blood sausage) for a few minutes on each side, until browned. Set aside on a plate.

Add another tbsp of oil to the pan and crack in the eggs. Cook until they are set but still a little runny in the middle.

Split the rolls and divide among four plates. Top each with some black pudding, squashing it down a little with a fork, then put an egg on top and season. Put the top on each roll so it's one big fat sandwich and dig in!

clever cooking

~ If you prefer to make this with bacon, grill (broil) a couple of rashers (strips) per person while you're frying the egg.

Storecupboard essentials

Cans of chopped tomatoes

Cans of chickpeas (garbanzo beans),
  red kidney beans and cannellini beans

Tomato purée (paste)

Tomato ketchup

Gherkins

Capers

Black olives

Anchovies

Olive oil

Vegetable oil

Sunflower oil

Toasted sesame oil

Groundnut (peanut) oil

White wine vinegar

Red wine vinegar

Balsamic vinegar

Mayonnaise

Dijon mustard

Horseradish sauce

Soy sauce

Chilli sauce

Worcestershire sauce

Red wine

Dry white wine

Pasta

Rice

Couscous

Polenta

Noodles

Vegetable, chicken, lamb and beef stock

English mustard powder

Cayenne pepper, cinnamon sticks, chilli
  powder, dried chilli flakes, fennel seeds,
  ground cinnamon, ground cloves,
  ground cumin, juniper berries, paprika,
  saffron, star anise, turmeric, whole
  cloves, whole nutmeg

Salt

Black peppercorns

Plain (all-purpose) flour

'00' pasta flour

Strong white bread flour

Baking powder

Fast-action dried yeast

Granulated (regular) sugar

Caster (superfine) sugar

Soft light brown sugar

Icing sugar

Almonds

Pine nuts

Walnuts

Golden syrup

Maple syrup

Dried fruits

Runny honey

Vanilla extract

Cocoa powder

Dark chocolate

Thank you, thank you...

Where do I begin? There are so many people I am grateful to. First, massive thanks to all the lovely personnes directly involved in the book, who helped make it happen seemingly so effortlessly and with such professionalism. They are Becca Spry, Emma Marsden (who went above and beyond), Chris Terry, Pene Parker, Lisa Harrison, Polly Powell, Georgie Hewitt, Charlotte Selby, Susan Fleming, my sis Kerry and my gorgeous boys Rory and Ewan (who take their recipes verrry seriously). And to all the unacknowledged beavers behind the scenes, many thanks to you as well.

Special thanks to Matthew, who has contributed to more than a few of the recipes and continues to be a culinary inspiration to me.

Thank you, gorgeous Elaine, for being there, always.

Thanks to my agents Debbie Catchpole and Verity O'Brien for their tenacity and tirelessness.

And in no particular order (apart from alphabetical), general eternal feelings of gratitude go to... Karen Barnes, James Berrington, James Campbell, Gemma Clarke, Jeff Cole, Kitty Corrigan, Georgina Davidson, Anne and Walter Dempster, Damien Doorley, Flic Everett, Anita Feldman, Emma Franklin, Chris Gates, Carol Gordon, Rachel Goulcher, Kevin Gratton, Steph Harris, Beth and John Hay, Lisa Hitchin, Jane Houghton, Amanda James, Josh Joseph, Julie Kitchener, Lidia Maj, Gill Morgan, Mum (aka Joan MacKenzie), Ronnie Murray, Lindsay Nicholson, Kim Placko, Liz Potter, Sarah Randell, Margaret Rooke, Helen Rose, Pete and Carol Stoddhart, Wendy Townsend, Ewan Venters, Pawel Waniewski, Alison Whyte and Mickey Yudkin.

And everyone else who's been kind to me about my cooking!